Kokoda Trek
75th Anniversary

Nikki Moyes

Copyright © 2017 Nikki Moyes

Photos © 2017 Nikki Moyes

All rights reserved.

This book or any portion thereof may not be reproduced or used in any manner whatsoever without the express written permission of the author except for the use of brief quotations in a book review.

Author: Moyes, Nikki

Title: **Kokoda Trek: 75th anniversary**/*Nikki Moyes*.

ISBN: 9780648146315 (paperback)

Subjects: World War, 1939-1945—Campaigns—Papua New Guinea.

World War, 1939-1945—Australia.

Kokoda Trail (Papua New Guinea) –History.

Papua New Guinea—Description and travel.

Introduction

Day 1 - Port Moresby to Kokoda to Hoi

Day 2 - Hoi to Isurava

Day 3 - Isurava to Templeton's Crossing 2

Day 4 - Templeton's Crossing 2 to Naduri

Day 5 - Naduri to Menari

Day 6 - The Sabbath

Day 7 - Menari to Nauro

Day 8 - Nauro to Ioribaiwa

Day 9 - Ioribaiwa to Goldie River

Day 10 - Goldie River to Owers' Corner

About the Trek

About the Author

Dedication

To my grandad, Dugald Moyes
1924 – 2009

To all the Australians who fought on the Kokoda Track in 1942 and to the Fuzzy Wuzzy Angels who made it possible.

Aussie Aussie song

Aussie Aussie, fought on this land
Fuzzy Wuzzy, the guiding hand
Steep are the hills we're climbing today
Rivers and valleys dividing the way
Mateship and courage, it's the Kokoda way
We've come a long way (long way from home)

- The porters' song

Introduction

The Kokoda Track (also known as Kokoda Trail) is a 96 kilometre track winding across the Owen Stanley Ranges in Papua New Guinea (PNG).

In 1942, the narrow track through the dense jungle was the scene of months of bitter fighting between Japanese and Australian troops, as the Japanese advanced over the mountains to capture the capital Port Moresby. From there it was believed they would launch an invasion of Australia.

The track has become a pilgrimage of sorts to Australians wanting to test themselves against the conditions our grandfathers fought in to protect our country during WWII. Some trekkers choose to carry all their gear for the 7-10 day trek in their pack as the soldiers had done, while others like myself elect to hire a native porter to carry the main pack so only a daypack is needed.

The mostly single-file track is so much more than steep hills, mud, and war memorials. The Kokoda Track passes over spectacular mountain terrain accessible only by walking and the occasional helicopter.

For those who love trekking, incredible plant life, and meeting people from different cultures, this is a journey of a lifetime.

A good level of fitness is required – some days we were on the track for ten hours. Many trekkers are evacuated off the track each year due to injury, sickness, or lack of fitness.

The track can be walked from north-south – the direction of the Australian soldiers' fighting withdrawal against the superior Japanese forces, or south-north – the direction of the Australians' advance back up the track to re-take Kokoda as the Japanese 'advanced to the rear'. I walked north-south on my trek with Back Track Adventures.

This is not a trek to do on your own. All the land is privately owned and companies require permission to run treks along the track. Also, in various locations, the trail disappeared; and without local trekking crew, it would have been difficult to find our way.

This is my story of trekking through the terrain my grandfather fought on 75 years ago, for the 2017 Anzac Day[1] trek.

Porters wait to help trekkers across a log bridge.

---

[1] For any non-Australian readers, Anzac stands for Australian and New Zealand Army Corp. Anzac Day is a day for remembrance in both Australia and New Zealand with many people attending a Dawn Service to honour those who fought for our countries.

Front cover photo - My porter Ben walked the track.

Back cover photo – cloud cover made the track misty.

Day 1 – Port Moresby to Kokoda to Hoi
17th April 2017

My trekking group arrived at the Port Moresby domestic terminal shortly after 5:00 am. The thirteen of us, including trek leader, Martin, and trainee leader, Carla, had been up since 4:00 am to make sure we were booked onto the flight early enough for our excess baggage to make the trip with us.

Another group of Australians, also destined for Kokoda and wearing shirts printed with #notdeadyet, were already waiting in the Papua New Guinea airport.

Martin joined us with a handful of plane tickets and the good news that all the gear made it onto the flight. The bad news was the flight time had changed and we had an extra two hours to wait.

I was anxious to get going. At 96 kilometres, the Kokoda Track would be the first overnight trek I'd ever done and it had a reputation for being challenging. I'd only started serious training four weeks earlier and I was eager to know if I was fit enough to complete the ten-day trek.

The later flight became delayed as the airport staff tried to find a working plane to fly us to the northern side of the Owen Stanley Mountain Range for the start of the trek.

We spent the time getting to know each other and it didn't take long before our lack of internet had us making up a list of things to Google as soon as we finished the trek. A couple of people still had their phones with them, but 'how many people have died walking the track' seemed best to find out after our return.

"We'll have run out of things to talk about before we even start walking," someone said.

"I've heard much of the track is single file so we won't have to talk to each other," Danni joked.

Four hours after our original flight time, we were ushered out to an old twin propeller Dash 8 plane. The staff only allowed our group and the other Australian trekking group to board. The replacement plane wasn't big enough for everyone else booked to fly to Popondetta – from where we would begin our journey to Kokoda.

We took our seats, noting the duct tape holding the inside of the plane together. Rachael made a comment about not liking 'small' planes.

As we began take-off, a guy from the other group proceeded to tell stories about plane issues he'd experienced during his time in the Airforce. Rachael, seated in front of him, giggled nervously.

Adrian leaned across the aisle with a nod towards the guy behind us. "He must be one of the ones Phil warned us about." I grinned and tried to give Rachael a reassuring smile.

The previous night we had a meeting where the company owner, Phil, gave us the run-down of the trek. He made it clear that when we met groups coming the other way on the track, we weren't to joke about what was ahead for them.

"You never know someone else's state of mind. Your comment may be what makes them give up," Phil said.

We flew over the mountain range we would be hiking, but I had an aisle seat and the clouds obscured the peaks, so I couldn't see what we would be facing.

We landed at Popondetta airport with all the duct tape still in place. A light rain had set in and we huddled under the airport shed roof while our bags were unloaded.

"I'm glad we're walking back to Port Moresby," Rachael muttered, giving the plane a final look.

Two army-style trucks with bench seats waited for us beside the barbed-wire fence. A couple of native trekking crew took our bags onto one, while we piled into the other tarp-covered truck.

A couple of uncomfortable bumpy hours later, we stopped in the middle of a two-lane bridge. Climbing out to stretch our legs and look at the river below, trek leader, Martin, informed us this was the location of one of the first encounters between the Australians and the Japanese in 1942, before the heavily outnumbered Australians fell back to defend Kokoda.

Kokoda Village only had a small airstrip, which was why we flew into Popondetta, but during WWII it was a valuable asset to defend. It also marked the northern end of the Kokoda Track.

From where we stood on the bridge, that still had a newly constructed look about it, we could see the smaller peaks of the mountain range ahead of us peeking out from beneath the clouds.

We climbed back into the truck for the second half of the journey. The narrow gravel road wound past locals harvesting palm fruits from the plantations.

As we crossed one bridge, a couple of children played in the shallow water beside a section of rusty caterpillar track that looked like it had come off an army tank.

By the time we arrived at Kokoda, the Garmin Vivo Fit2 I wore on my wrist had racked up 6,000 steps from the bumpy truck ride.

We were four hours behind schedule, but the first day only had a two-hour walk scheduled. We piled out of the truck and Martin whisked us away for a quick look around the Kokoda Museum, with its information boards about the WWII battles (written in both English and Pidgin English) and various rusty guns and helmets.

I didn't have enough time to process the experience of seeing weapons used to defend our country[2] 75 years ago before Martin called us outside to have a brief look at the memorials.

Four white memorial stones encircled one edge of a grassy oval. We conducted a brief walk past taking photos to look at later when we had time. The stones were dedicated to those who fought here 75 years ago, including one for the native carriers known as Fuzzy Wuzzy Angels who carried supplies and wounded for the Australians, and one stone with Japanese writing.

---

[2] Papua New Guinea was an Australian territory in 1942.

Looking back towards where we left the trucks and our packs, blue-grey mountains rose from the clouds. Beneath them sat the village houses with their corrugated iron roofs and louvre windows. We saw a couple of villagers, but none of them interacted with us.

A brief trip to the toilet hut revealed a long drop with a seat and lid — BYO toilet paper and hand sanitiser. With the door shut, it was difficult to see where anything was.

Nicole revealed the toilet-ranking system she'd developed over years of travelling. One star was given for every luxury, so a star for each of the following: a toilet, toilet paper, a place to wash hands, soap, and a place for drying hands.

We hurried back to our packs, as we needed to start walking soon to make our first campsite. Martin read out the names of the personal porters we were matched with. Mine shook my hand and rattled off a long name. I stared at him blankly.

"Ben," he said. I sighed in relief. I'm terrible at remembering names, but Ben was simple.

He grabbed my big pack and set about packing his tiny bag and extra camp supplies in the top, while I tried to work out how to adjust my hiking poles to the correct height.

Trainee leader, Carla, came to my rescue, helping me set them at the right height and pointing out that the rubber boots came off the end leaving a spike that would be useful in the mud.

I'd never hiked with poles or a pack before, so I was still feeling flustered when Martin called out for packs on. I hurriedly pulled my gaiters on over my hiking boots before he led us towards the arch marking the start of the Kokoda Track. Several letters had fallen off, so it read, "KO DA TRAI".

We took a few minutes to pose for photos under the arch before our native trek leader, Vicko, started what would become a familiar morning call:

"Are we ready?"

"YES!" shouted the rest of the trekking crew.
"Are we ready?" Vicko repeated.
"YES!" (Crew.)
"Ten seconds!"
"9-8-7-6-5-4-3-2-1!"
"Who are we?"
"Back Track!"
"What is our profession?"
(Everyone.) "Bo Bo Ba Ba! Let's go, rock and roll!"

Vicko headed off down a set of muddy vehicle tracks and we fell in behind him. Our personal porters took up positions beside each of us, while Martin and Carla walked at the rear.

I ended up near the back of the group as my short legs struggled to keep pace with the others. My new hiking poles felt awkward in my hands, so I carried them as we walked. I briefly considered tucking them into my bag, but that would have involved stopping and I was already falling behind the main group.

I made myself focus solely on today instead of the whole ten-day trek ahead of us. All I had to get through was two hours walking and we would stop for camp.

About ten minutes in, we passed a group walking the other way. It was a surprise to encounter a team finishing so early in the month. April, being the tail-end of the Wet Season, is generally the wettest[3] and therefore most difficult time to walk the track, but it's popular for people wanting to be on the track for Anzac Day. That was still eight days away.

Their Australian leader paused briefly for a chat with someone he knew from our group. He said he was turning around when he reached Kokoda and walking the 96 km track back in the other direction the following day. For our group just beginning to venture into the unknown, the idea of back-to-back treks was unthinkable.

---

[3] Most treks operate between April and October to avoid the main Wet Season. Of course, being a mountain range, it can rain any time of year.

We continued on. The first section of track facing us was reasonably flat, although the sloppy mud meant making good time was a challenge.

Vicko wore hiking boots like us, but a couple of the Papua New Guinea boys were barefoot and my guy, Ben wore thongs on his feet.

Ben and I chatted briefly. He said he was married with two children. I replied that I was single and lived with my cat. Ben's village was not along the track. If I understood correctly, his family lived somewhere to the east. As neither of us seemed adept at small talk, the conversation died off fairly quickly after that.

After almost two hours, the vehicle tracks disappeared and we encountered a small, damp log lying across a narrow creek. Ben stepped into the water and held my hand[4] as I crossed the log. The creek must see a lot of rain because there was a second higher and larger log balanced across two boulders a few metres away.

Ten minutes later, we emerged from the trees onto a well-kept grassy area. The red of leaves and flowers brightened the greens of the jungle. The scattered huts were traditionally made from wood, bark, and pandanus leaves.

We crossed another shallow creek, this one with rocks just breaking the surface for us to walk along. Ben took hold of my elbow as I picked my way across the wet stones. Another few minutes and we arrived in the village campsite of Hoi. The actual village huts must have been set away from the track as we didn't encounter any locals.

It was about 4:30 pm when the porters began to set up camp. We discovered that we each had our own tent to sleep in, which felt like the best news we'd had all day. Despite only walking for two hours, we were ready for our long day to be over.

---

[4] Phil had mentioned that the boys would do this for their trekkers as their way of keeping us safe and injury free and that we shouldn't refuse if they offered a hand.

Ben pitched my tent among the others on the grass, took his stuff out of the top of the pack and left me to make my bed. I chose to bring an inflatable camp mat and pillow on the trek, instead of a light foam mat, to make sure I slept well each night. The two-man tent was just big enough to fit me and my pack inside.

I changed into my bathers and sandals, and headed back to the last creek to wash. Ben appeared like a shadow behind me just as I missed a stepping stone on the track and my right foot sunk ankle deep into a muddy puddle. I shook the muck off my foot and kept walking. Ben monitored me like an overprotective babysitter the rest of the way to the creek.

Ron and Andrew had the same idea as me and I joined them in the refreshing water. I rinsed out the clothes I'd worn that day, before heading back to camp, this time managing to avoid the mud puddle.

The campsite consisted of an open hut with a dirt floor, wooden table and benches, and a hut with a raised timber floor where the trekking crew slept. There was a blue-painted hut and another half built with exposed timber structure nearby, but we didn't see the village residents while we were there.

The PNG boys[5] served us dinner in the open hut. That night was a pot of mashed potato, a pot of curried sausages, and chicken noodle soup that looked like it came out of packets.

Mealtimes turned out not to be simple. Rachael was celiac, Felicity was vegetarian and had allergies, and Nicole 'didn't eat mammals'[6]. It was lean pickings for them, even though they'd declared special dietary needs before the trip.

---

[5] Martin informed us the native trekking crew were affectionately referred to as 'the boys'. It is not an insult as it can be in other cultures and we all had great respect for these descendants of the Fuzzy Wuzzy Angels who cared for the Australian soldiers during WWII.

[6] A weird description, but that's how she described her diet. She was happy to eat chicken or fish.

Light rain set in by the time dinner was over and the grass became slick with mud, making it difficult to keep our footing as we left the hut.

One of the porters pulled out a machete to cut gullies around a tent to prevent the rain flooding it during the night.

Carla had brought an umbrella[7] and offered to share it as we made our way to the toilet by the light of our torches. The hut had three walls and no door. The long drop didn't have a raised seat like in Kokoda. It consisted of a vagina-shaped hole in the ground, approximately the size I'd imagine one to be after birthing a large baby. Not the easiest thing to negotiate in the dark.

Carla stood sentry while I carefully completed my business, managing not to drop my torch or fall in. When I was finished, I stepped outside and held the umbrella while Carla took her turn. We made it back to the camp without incident.

I crawled into my tent and checked how many steps I'd done for the day. My Garmin showed 23,602, but about 6,000 of those were from the bumpy truck ride. I turned off my torch and curled up on my inflatable mat to sleep. The night was still warm and humid so I'd left my sleeping bag off.

A drop of water landed on my leg. Moments later another followed. I moved my mat as far to one side of the tent as it would go, but I was still being dripped on. I felt around in the dark, but couldn't find the cause of the problem without leaving the tent. I finally found a rubbish bag in my gear and pulled it over my leg to keep dry.

Just as I got comfortable again, a drip sounded by my head. I switched my torch back on and discovered the fly touching the end of my tent letting water seep through. I unzipped the flyscreen and propped one of my sandals against it so it was no longer touching.

---

[7] This was a tip Martin shared with her. Rain jackets are useless on the track as the humidity makes you sweaty, however a small umbrella can be useful around the campsite.

I curled up again and was about to drift off to sleep when a machete hit the wet ground inches from my tent, startling me fully awake.

I lay in my bed listening to the sounds of the machete and rain and wondered about the soldiers fighting on the track 75 years ago.

Many of the Australians during the beginning of the Kokoda Campaign didn't even have a ground sheet to sleep on. They would have spent many wet nights huddled in their foxholes waiting for the day to begin so they could continue fighting.

Above: The trucks we rode in from Popondetta to Kokoda Village.

Left: Sign at Kokoda Village.

Top: A mountain peeking out from above the clouds behind Kokoda Village.

Below: Starting the trek at Kokoda Village.

Top: The start of the track was flat and wide enough for a vehicle.

Below: A water crossing before our first campsite at Hoi.

Day 2 – Hoi to Isurava
18th April 2017

Martin's rooster impersonation woke us at 5:00 am. He'd obviously practiced it on many occasions; however the village roosters took objection to it and attempted to out-crow him.

As I fumbled in the dark for my torch, the porters began singing a beautiful melody from their hut. I couldn't make out the words, but they were quite talented singers.

I packed my belongings by torch light and temporarily lost my camera in the process, making me one of the last to reach the dining hut for breakfast.

We had a big pot of water for making tea, coffee, or milo; a pot of porridge, cereal, and bananas. I didn't normally eat porridge, but I poured honey on top and ate it while the porters packed up our tents.

Nicole announced a change to her toilet ranking system as her current one didn't hold up to Kokoda Track conditions. Now there was a star for: a door, a toilet (as opposed to a hole in the ground), a toilet seat, toilet paper, and somewhere to wash hands.

Mist had settled around us giving the morning an eerie feeling. We shouldered our packs and waited for the whole team to be ready.

I pointed out to Rachael and Felicity that the rubber stoppers come off the ends of the hiking poles[8]. We passed the message around the group as Matthew appeared to be the only other person who knew about it.

As we'd been rushed yesterday due to the delayed flight, Martin arranged for us to officially meet all the trekking crew before we set off for the day. We made a line and the boys filed past us pausing to shake our hands and say their name.

---

[8] The poles had a metal point to the end (under the rubber stopper) that was useful to dig into mud for extra grip. It was extremely helpful on the wet and slippery track.

Many were soft spoken so I didn't catch everyone's name, but there were several of the same names, to the point where I was sure there were at least three Jeremys. Trekker Danni was matched with porter Danny, while her father, Adrian was matched with porter Adrian.

The trekking crew consisted of twenty boys, including leader Vicko and ten personal porters. The rest carried the trek supplies and would also keep an eye on the three trekkers who elected to carry a full pack and therefore didn't have a personal porter.

I worked out that Ben always wore a white, blue and red hat, which made it easier for me to pick him out quickly from the rest of the group all wearing blue Back Track Adventures shirts.

Around 6:30 am, Vicko started the *'are we ready'* call and we set off. I fell in behind Vicko with Rachael behind me. The porters slotted in between, ready to grab us if we slipped on the wet ground. Vicko had a smaller pack than the other porters, but his had a large coil of blue rope hanging off the back and I wondered if it was to rescue us if we fell off the edge of the track.

Ben walked barefoot that day. The track was single file and for the first hour, we climbed about 300 metres in altitude. Vicko paused every twenty minutes or so for us to rest our burning calves and drink some water. The back of the group caught up, generally only about five minutes behind the rest of us at each stop. We were hot from climbing, but the mist hung around keeping the tropical jungle temperature bearable.

Martin and Carla remained at the rear, encouraging the slower members of the group and making sure no one was left behind. Most kept pace with me. I have short legs so it wasn't that difficult for them. Vicko strolled slowly ahead of me like he was out for a walk with small children who wouldn't be able to keep up if he walked at his normal speed.

After an hour and a half, we emerged from the thick jungle and clouds, over a small rise and entered a large sunny clearing with carefully mown lawns.

The area was Deniki village campsite. It had the open dining hut and the raised-floor hut for the trekking crew, as well as two small huts for the long drops[9]. The village houses were on a different levelled clearing and we didn't go near them.

The sunny clearing opened out to views of the surrounding mountains. On a clear day, Kokoda and its tiny airstrip could be seen, but that morning cloud blanketed the valley.

At Deniki, where in 1942 the heavily outnumbered[10] Australians withdrew when they could no longer hold the Kokoda airstrip from the advancing Japanese, I had my first profound moment of the trek.

"Why has no one ever told me how beautiful this place is? Everyone always just talks about how hard this trek is!" I repeated this to everyone in hearing until they edged away under the pretence of taking photos of the spectacular views. I was aware that we still had another seven hours walking ahead of us for the day, but in that moment I felt like I could achieve anything.

The whoop whoop sound of a helicopter interrupted my moment. The red bird circled overhead before coming down to rest just out of eyesight on another plateau below us.

The porters ran to have a look at it land, while a lone man and his porter, who were in the dining hut when we arrived, made their way down also.

"It's like the *Hunger Games*," Nicole announced. "Cannon shots fired in the sky to mark the first casualty of the track." Those of us who had read or watched '*The Hunger Games*' nodded along in agreement as we witnessed our first evacuation[11] from the track.

---

[9] This was standard for each campsite along the track. The bigger villages had multiple campsites each with the same setup.

[10] The original Australian force numbered around 100 men.

[11] When I got home, I Googled evacuations and came back with a figure of around 50 trekkers per year. We heard the helicopter several times every day we were on the track.

Vicko called out, "*Let's rock and roll*," and we shouldered our day packs again. I glanced at my Garmin, but it said I'd only done 2,000 steps[12]. I took my position up front again, preferring to set the pace rather than fall behind the main group like on the first day.

We headed uphill once more and this time I was glad for my hiking poles. They dug into the wet ground and stopped me losing my footing on the steep sections of narrow track. My thighs and calves burned with the effort, but my Grandad was here in 1942 and his entire life he insisted that downhill was harder. I kept that in mind as I focused on putting my feet in the same places Ben did.

There was a brief downhill section before we encountered an almost level piece of track winding along the gently sloping side of a mountain. Both sides were covered in a dense green vine that grabbed at my poles as I passed.

When Matthew asked about the weed-like vine, Vicko said the Japanese soldiers brought it here, probably as part of their jungle camouflage[13].

The trees were sparse and tall here, becoming denser further off the track, and the occasional flowering bush captured my attention with its wide, pale purple petals or dainty red flowers. When I looked ahead, the track disappeared among the waist high foliage.

Our next rest stop was beside a little creek and Ben collected my water bottle to fill from the stream for me. Conversation flowed around water tasting like iodine or chlorine depending on the purification tablets used to treat the water. Rachael and I had gone with a UV light option, which left the refreshing water taste untainted. It was also quicker,

---

[12] I had it on my wrist and as I was taking several steps for each time I moved my hiking poles, it wasn't recording my actual steps.

[13] The Japanese were experienced in jungle warfare and would use camouflage making them difficult to see. The Australians had a 'desert' uniform. The yellow made them stand out among the green of the jungle and the shorts did nothing to protect them from sharp-edged grasses or biting insects.

taking about a minute with the light in the water as opposed to the tablets that were meant to sit in the water for half an hour before drinking.

We sat down to wait for the tail end of the group and honey bees settled on our shirts, drinking the sweat from our backs. Other bees crawled over the damp rocks, collecting water to take back to their wild hives. With the amount of bees we encountered on the track, I was surprised I never saw any of the villagers keeping hives.

"How are you going with the pack?" I asked Matt. He, Andrew, and Ron had all chosen to carry the full pack instead of a day bag.

"Good," he replied way too cheerily for someone who had been carrying seventeen kilograms on his back while hiking up the side of a mountain.

"I'm doing good with mine as well," I teased, motioning to my day bag with my water and snacks inside.

"That's not a pack!" Matt replied.

"It's forty litres." I stated the bag capacity, although it was lucky to weigh five kilograms even with all the water I was carrying.

"I've seen bigger Louis Vuitton bags," Andrew joked.

Martin arrived behind the others and the porters hurried to fill their trekkers' water bottles while Martin lay down on the track. I was a bit disappointed he wasn't providing details about the Kokoda Campaign as we travelled. Luckily I'd read a couple of books before coming, so I knew the rough details of the Australians' fighting withdrawal.

I didn't know much about the Australian advance back up the track though, which I believed is where Grandad joined the Campaign as a translator. History books seem to prefer to focus on the initial heroics of the outnumbered and under-trained men, than the equally bloody battles to reclaim the land back from the invaders.

Martin climbed to his feet and we set off again heading mostly uphill. The rain during the night made the track slippery and Ben monitored me closely to ensure I remained on my feet.

I stopped to take a photo when we reached a tiny creek crossing. Vicko and Ben waited patiently until I was ready to be helped across the wet rocks.

When we paused again, my Garmin displayed 6,000 steps despite us having walked for several hours. I asked the rest of the group for a count. Matthew's Fitbit watch had 15,000. Nicole's pedometer had 13,500. Andrew's phone had 10,500, but it appeared to be low due to the phone being in power saving mode.

I took mine off my wrist and tied it through my shoelace in the hopes of a more accurate reading. My gaiter just reached over the top, keeping it and my laces reasonably clean of the mud coating my hiking boots.

"I'm really hungry. Is it nearly lunch time?" Rachael asked.

"No," I said, checking my watch.

"What time is it anyway?" Andrew asked.

"10:20 am," I said. It felt like we'd been walking for hours. I did a quick calculation – actually we had been walking for almost four hours.

"Why would you tell us that? I don't want to know the time unless it's lunch time," Rachael declared.

"Sorry," I said unapologetically.

We continued walking and having breaks for another hour before we stopped for lunch. While the PNG boys served up two-minute noodles, I removed my boots.

I don't like wearing footwear, and living in a tropical city, I manage to avoid doing so much of the time[14]. After a whole morning of walking, my feet were white[15] and showing signs of wrinkles, especially on my little toes.

One of my socks had slipped and my right heel was beginning to rub. The second toe on my left foot had a blister

---

[14] Yes, I even walk around the office barefoot.
[15] Okay, whiter than normal. I'm one of those people who doesn't tan.

forming under the nail. I let my feet air while I ate. It felt great until I had to put my sweaty socks and boots back on.

The afternoon continued the same as the morning. Some sections were so steep, Ben had to reach down and help me up. Sometimes there were creek crossings[16] and in other places the muddy track hugged the steep drop-off of the mountain ridge.

I spent a lot of time comparing the terrain to bushwalks in Australia. First of all, no Australian walk would be open to the public in this condition. Many national parks close to visitors during the tropical North's Wet Season, so not to be damaged by vehicles or trekkers.

Secondly, there were no timber steps or purposely placed stones to make the steep sections manageable. Most of the time I watched the ground and Ben's feet, but whenever I remembered to look up, the scenery was amazing – tall green jungle, glimpses of mountain views, and spectacular flowers.

We were under the jungle canopy much of the time. When I was younger, my grandad said that during WWII, he never saw anyone he fired his gun[17] at. I'd naively assumed that he hadn't been near the enemy.

Walking the track Dugald Moyes fought on 75 years earlier, I realised it was because you wouldn't see the enemy in this jungle until you were on top of them, something the porters demonstrated days later when they played a joke on us.

We eventually climbed up over another rise into the biggest village I'd seen since leaving Kokoda. Families watched us as we took a moment to look back over the mountains behind us.

---

[16] I took photos of the first few, before realising there would be too many to continue doing that and I saved my photo stops for the more spectacular views.

[17] As he was a translator instead of a soldier, he was only provided with two dozen rounds that he kept in his handkerchief. I assume he had an officer's pistol instead of the larger rifle.

Vicko waited for us to keep moving. This was the new Isurava Village. It had moved further along the track from its 1942 position. We continued on, only to stop for a water break a few minutes later by the village campsite.

Another trekking team was being briefed on the war history by their team leader inside a dining hut. They moved on shortly after we arrived. Martin hadn't shared much with us yet, despite this being his eleventh trek and his grandfather being one of the original 39th Battalion soldiers who defended this country against the Japanese invasion.

We flopped down on a grassy area in sight of the dining hut. The day's journey had been steep, increasing in altitude by over 800 metres. The rear end of the group arrived and Martin collapsed on the ground, his shirt soaked with sweat. Anthony also took the opportunity to lie down. We still had hours of walking ahead of us to reach our scheduled campsite at Alola Village.

"While everyone's here, I have some of my grandad's documents to share," I addressed the group sitting or lying in various stages of recovery around me.

Dugald Moyes turned eighteen in June 1942 and having taught himself to read Japanese characters, he become part of the newly-formed Allied Translator and Interpreter Service. He was still in Australia during the initial fighting withdrawal by our soldiers and I believe he arrived on the track as the Australians began the pushback towards Kokoda.

Grandad passed away a few years ago which was when my brother found wartime documents among his belongings, some appearing to be from the War Trials in Rabaul.

I pulled out the first document I brought with me. The Japanese characters were neat and precise. Grandad's translation was cursive and hard to decipher. I read it out to the group.

Reference Patrolling Instructions
Facts which ought to be born in mind.

1. The welfare of the whole army is carried on the shoulders of those with a strong sense of duty.
2. Normally the stress on the mind causes a want to discontinue the action and it becomes dangerous to the concentration.
3. Normally in the jungle, the enemy is discovered very near at hand. Superior enemy forces and difficult terrain does not authorise retreat as it could lead to annihilation (enemy has automatic rifles). Tactics become one of extreme stubborn defence.
4. Unit Commanders make and receive situation reports but if it becomes impossible, Commanders are to make arbitrary decisions to do their duty when face-to-face with the enemy.
5. Negligence becomes a powerful enemy. If the enemy is thrusting forward, resistive action gives quick mastery when defending ground.

I tucked the page back into my bag and Matt asked everyone how they went getting the medical done for the hike.

Felicity's doctor said she wouldn't make it. Her father, Anthony, was told he'd be fine as his legs worked. The doctor ignored the arthritis in his neck and shoulders.

Danni's doctor hadn't seen her before and said he'd believe she was fit. Andrew's told him he was fitter than the last bloke he saw and stamped his form 'approved'.

The doctor I saw was Indian and had never heard of Kokoda. The letter provided with the medical form had **'hiking in high heat and humidity'** typed in bold. This was normal weather for where I live.

"So you'll be outside?" the doctor asked. "Make sure you drink plenty of water." He approved my form without even asking what exercise I normally do.

Martin eventually roused himself. He was pale and covered in sweat. "As you are all aware, I'm not well. So we're going to be stopping early today."

Rachael and I glanced at each other. We'd been at the front of the group so hadn't realised Martin was sick.

"He's been vomiting all day," Felicity leaned in to tell us.

Our new campsite would be at the Isurava battle site. Vicko called *'rock and roll'* and we headed off. By our map, there was a Japanese plane crash site, forty-five minutes of steep climb off the main track. Because Martin was sick and we were travelling slower than predicted, we passed by it. That's the nature of the track. Plans change and we had to be ready to adapt to changing circumstances.

The terrain undulated up and down. At one point we descended rapidly to a wide creek. Tree branches had been cut down to form a bridge with a few wedged in upright to hold it together.

Vicko went first, unwinding his coil of blue rope to tie as a grab rail. When it was secure, I started across with Ben holding on to the back of my bag in case I slipped on the uneven footings. I made it safely to the other side only to have the track ascend sharply ahead of me.

I followed Vicko up, before we stopped so Vicko could check everyone had crossed safely. Rachael's porter, Stephan let go of her hand before she was completely across, thinking she was fine. Rachael paused for a second to see if she could make it across on her own. Ben yelled out something to Stephan and he quickly took her hand again. She made it across safely and joined me up on the track.

The trekking crew carrying the camp supplies moved ahead of us on the narrow track. One of the young boys carrying a full pack lost his footing as he moved around Vicko. He slid over the edge, catching himself with his arms on the edge of the track. He hauled himself back up, grinning sheepishly. Luckily, he was uninjured, although I'm sure he would have been teased by the other porters about it later that day.

By 2:30 pm, we approached old Isurava where we'd be staying the night. Carla said our original campsite at Alola was another three hours walk.

As we came down the steep descent into the village, one of my feet slipped out from under me. Ben was in front of me, but Rachael's porter, Stephen grabbed the back of my pack and I landed gently on my behind.

"I'm fine," I called out so Ben didn't worry. I got carefully to my feet and Ben took hold of my arm until the ground became flatter – no longer trusting me to stay upright.

We came across the first of the plaques describing the war history along the track:

> 1942   Isurava   1992
>
> The original Isurava Village located near here, was defended by 50 Papuans and 1,000 Australians against 6,000 Japanese. The Japanese who had just captured Kokoda Village, attacked Isurava from three directions; the high ground to the west, directly along the Kokoda Trail and 3 kilometres to the east on the other side of Eora Creek (660 metres below here).
>
> The thin Australian line held on all fronts despite continual attack between 26 to 30 August 1942. Australia's first Victoria Cross of the South-West Pacific was won here by Private Bruce Kingsbury on the 29 Aug.
>
> Eventually the overwhelming Japanese numbers, especially in the west, forced the Australians to withdraw towards Alola. The battle of Isurava lost the Japanese four valuable days and a great number of casualties. Both these factors ultimately contributed to their retreat on the hills above Port Moresby.

The red helicopter sat up on a plateau above where the porters began to set up our tents. We joked that we should run up there to ask the pilot to wait for Martin, but it took off before the tail end of our group arrived.

Once our tents were up and we'd sorted our beds for the night, Rachael, Felicity, and I walked over to the Isurava memorial.

The Australian and Papua New Guinean flags hung from poles beside four granite pillars with the words: courage, endurance, mateship, sacrifice, around a neatly maintained circle of gravel.

Further down the hill behind this were information boards about the 1942 battles on this location. As the 39th were about to be overrun, the 2/14th Battalion arrived, boosting the Australian numbers to 1,000 men. Despite the exhausting trek over the mountain range, they threw themselves straight into the battle against the Japanese.

Down the hill was another plaque, this one for Private Bruce Kingsbury VC[18] for his actions on this hill in repelling the Japanese who broke through the Australian lines. After charging the Japanese, he died from a sniper shot while reloading his gun.

The hill where the battle had taken place, had been cleared to make way for the memorial. Mown lawns replaced battle scars, making it difficult to image what it would have been like 75 years ago. Not a bullet remained, although porter Stephan had stepped on an old shell casing on the track earlier that day.

Felicity, Rachael, and I sat on the steps below the memorial and watched the clouds roll through the valley. They moved quickly, so by the time we'd taken photos, the clouds had obscured part of the valley visible moments earlier. It was peaceful and I enjoyed being able to stop and appreciate our surroundings.

Felicity had been sick a couple of weeks before the trek and had been worried about not being able to come. She didn't look like she was quite back to full strength and as a vegetarian with some food allergies, her diet had not been ideal since the trek started.

---

[18] Victoria Cross recipient.

She was more worried about her father though. Anthony had two porters helping him and they carried his day pack as well as the full pack. Vicko had assured Felicity that they'd get him over the track.

We were doing this hike as a charity challenge to raise money for Lifeline and Beyondblue. The company that coordinated between the charities and the trekking company, assured her there would be a vehicle to ride in if she or her dad struggled to keep up with the group.

Rachael and I looked at her in disbelief. Apart from the vehicle tracks at the very beginning of the hike, there was no way anything other than the helicopter could reach people in this jungle.

During WWII, the idea of a road through the Owen Stanley Ranges had been suggested. It was deemed impossible to achieve and 75 years later, the villagers use the same narrow hiking tracks as they did before the war.

After our long day, we were happy to camp at Isurava, but there was concern about the extra three hours we needed to make up due to stopping early.

We headed back to camp and took it in turns to use the shower[19]. The doorway was open to the view overlooking the toilets further down the hill. Several stones sat under the water flow, but you had to step through thick, dark mud to reach them.

The water was cold, but refreshing and I managed to get my clothes back on without covering myself in too much mud.

The porters served up popcorn before dinner and we sat around the dining hut eating it out of mugs with salt. Carla picked up the pot to pass around and got thick, black soot all over her palm.

"I'm so hungry," Rachael said, munching on the popcorn.

We joked about her wanting lunch at 10:20 am.

---

[19] A pipe with cold water flowing constantly through it protruded over the plateau below our campsite, obscured behind three thick black plastic walls.

"Nikki keeps telling me the time!" she exclaimed. "I left my watch at home on purpose."

"Sorry," I said. "It's a quarter to six, by the way."

Martin joined us after resting in his tent. When asked how he was, he said he was feeling about seventy percent. Carla held up her sooty hand and offered him the popcorn.

"Are you waiting for it to blow off?" he asked about the soot.

We ate a dinner of tomato pasta, a vegetable mix, and a pot of soup. Rachael got a special pot of vegetables. Her porter came over earlier to check if she could eat ginger so they could make her something. This became the basis for every dinner she got the rest of the trip.

Martin barely touched the food and disappeared back into his tent while we pored over his map of the track. There was a section ahead marked, 'steep steep' followed by, 'lots of leeches'[20].

"What do you think 'steep steep' is?" Rachael asked.

"We probably didn't want to know," I replied.

I was focused to taking each day as it came. So far it was working and I wasn't concerned about the distance still ahead of us.

The conversation moved on to our various aches and pains and I realised I'd been meaning to pack my spiky physio ball to get the knots out of my back. I'd completely forgotten about it until that moment.

Matthew gave us an odd look when we mentioned spiky balls and Andrew explained what it was used for.

"I put it against the wall and do this." He mimed rolling a ball up and down with his back against the thick wooden post of the dining hut.

"Is that even legal?" Matthew asked, making Andrew stop due to laughter.

"In ACT[21] it is," he fired back.

---

[20] Surprisingly, we didn't see any leeches the whole trek.
[21] We had a high portion of the group hailing from Canberra, Andrew being one of them.

"You're the odd one out here, Matthew," I said. "Three of us own spiky balls."

Matthew shook his head at us. "So what happens on the track goes on FaceTube, right?"

"Something like that." We didn't correct him, assuming he didn't have social media.

The PNG boys came back to collect the dishes and left us two packets of Tim Tams. We sat around the light of a small lantern and watched fireflies dart over the lawn.

It was a slippery walk down to the toilet in the dark, but at least it had a raised seat and a sheet of plastic for a door. We were in bed before 8 pm.

I pulled out my nail clippers[22] and trimmed back all my toe nails. The blister under one nail eventually made the nail die and fall off, but I didn't get any more like it.

My Garmin said I'd done a puny 15,733 steps and I threw it into a corner of the tent in disgust.

---

[22] This was a handy tip from my boss who does a bit of trekking. If a toenail is too long, it rubs on the boots especially if the terrain is steep.

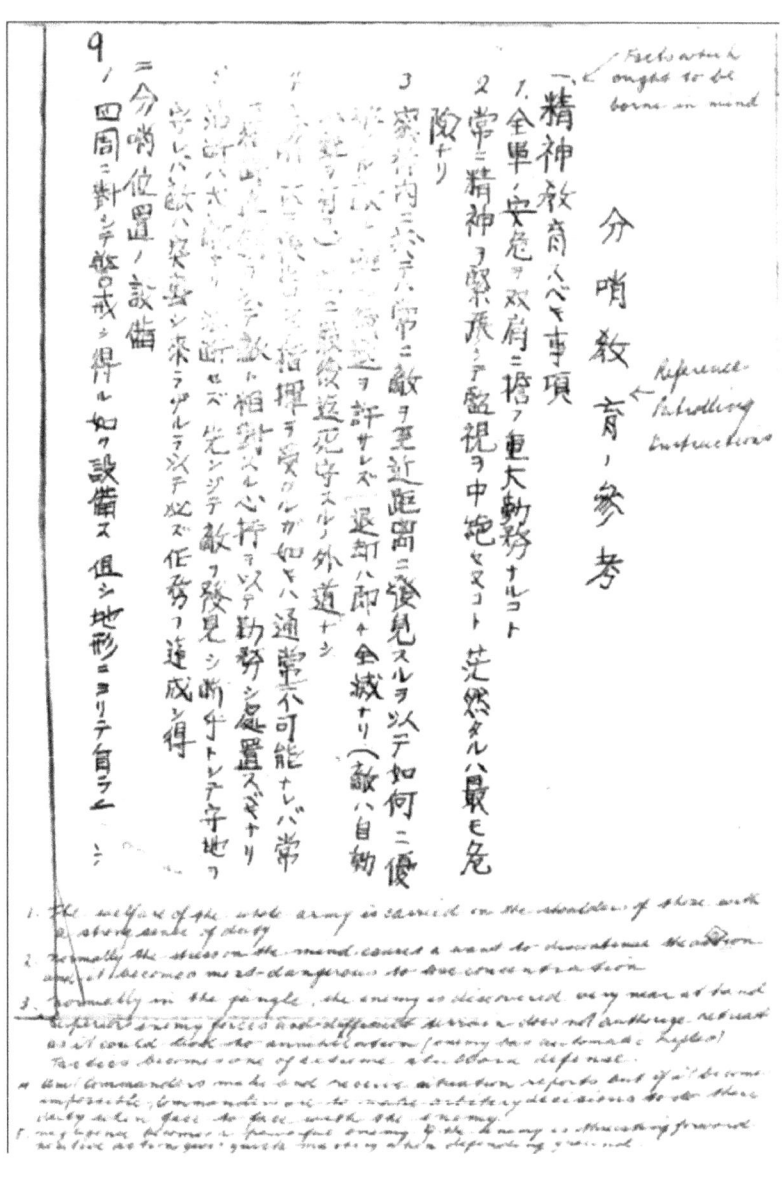

Japanese document translated by Dugald Moyes.

Top Left: A typical dining hut for trekkers, surrounded by an early morning mist, Hoi Village.

Top Right: The first sighting of the evacuation helicopter.

Below: Grassy campsite area at Deniki.

Left: Vicko waits for me to stop taking photos so we can keep walking. The track could barely be seen ahead of us.

Right: Vines carpet the jungle. Vicko said the vine came from the Japanese camouflage uniforms during WWII.

Left: A small stream the porters filled our water bottles from.

Below: Streams regularly cut across the narrow track.

Left: The view from one of the many mountain peaks.

Right: A glimpse of the next village in the distance.

Below: We climbed down one mountain, crossed the creek via a collection of small logs tied together, and then climbed back up the side of the next ridge.

Left: Second sighting of the helicopter, this time at Isurava.

Above: Isurava Memorial looking back down the valley towards Kokoda. The Australians held this hill for four days against the advancing Japanese in 1942.

Day 3 – Isurava to Templeton's Crossing 2
19th April 2017

Martin managed his rooster call at 5:00 am although it didn't sound as healthy as the day before. Over breakfast, we had a quick look at our map of the track and it showed we were only one hour and forty-five minutes away from where we were meant to camp last night. That cheered us up as Carla had said it would take three hours. We assumed she was taking into account Martin's pace.

After breakfast, Martin took us over to the memorial to tell us a bit about what happened here 75 years ago. I read a couple of books before I came on the trek, so the details were familiar to me. Ron stepped forward and read out a poem called, *'A Soldier's Farewell to His Son'*, while we contemplated the sacrifices made on this ground.

Clouds had settled into the valley, so the views were not as spectacular as they were the day before. We took a group photo by the four granite pillars before getting ready for another day hiking.

The porters had the camp packed up and we set off uphill once more. I was less stiff than I expected and after a few minutes I was walking normally, but by the first water break, my calves and thighs were burning.

The terrain became ridiculously steep and as I concentrated on getting my foot up to a point higher than my knee so I could take the next step, Rachael called out from below me.

"Do you think this is 'steep steep'?"

I laughed because I'd been thinking the same thing. "I hope so. I'd hate to see anything steeper," I replied.

At the peak of the ridge, we came upon a small village. The porters sat down and took off their packs. A wooden signpost beside us declared, *'welcome to Conn's Rock – WWII operation theatre ** for visit K10 per head'*.

Ten kina is approximately five Australian dollars. Despite being half the value, the currency was clearly influenced by Australia[23] with each numerical value having the same colour scheme as our own money.

The tail end of another trekking group was preparing to leave and their harassed leader approached us to ask who our leader was. Martin and Carla had yet to appear, but he caught sight of Matthew who he apparently knew. He pointed out a new sign stuck to a tree. An old PNG man stood beside it.

'Public Notic (sic)
* Check Point 1
Pay K100 – per head for each trekkers (sic)
NB – we collect our share of the Trek fee from the K.T.A.[24] as our Land Royalty.'

The Kokoda Track is not a National Park, instead owned entirely by native landholders, each with a claim over a different section of the track. It's like going for a walk through the backyards of a dozen extended families.

"Matthew, this man's grandson has put up this new sign. He wants a fee for passing through Alola Village."

"I'm not the trek leader," Matthew interrupted.

"Yes, but we need to get moving. I've sorted out our group, but you'll need to make your own arrangements regarding the fee," the stressed man said before hurrying off with the last of his group.

Carla arrived minutes later and we passed on the message. She glanced at the sign. "Stanley's already made the necessary arrangements," she said.

Stanley, our native PNG company man, had sorted everything before we arrived. After the stress caused by the

---

[23] Papua New Guinea was an Australian territory until becoming an independent country in 1975.
[24] The Kokoda Track Authority (KTA) manages the Kokoda Track for tourists, while improving the way of life for communities living along the track, through funding and development programmes.

other leader, we had no issues and didn't need to find any additional money to continue through the next village.

Martin arrived and led us down to Conn's Rock, the K10 per head having been arranged earlier and covered by our overall trek fee.

"Feels weird walking without poles," Danni said.

We'd left our packs and porters up on the track as we made our way down the short descent. I briefly wondered if I should have held onto my poles[25], but we all made it down without mishap.

We gathered around a large flat rock decorated with purple/pink leaves and red flowers from a native flowering bush.

A plaque dedicated to Butch Bisset[26], who died at this spot in the arms of his brother Stan[27], was surrounded by various rusting war memorabilia. Rusty Japanese and Australian helmets and water flasks were positioned by a coil of green signal wire.

The signal wire was laid along the track in 1942 and was the only way of communicating with Port Moresby Headquarters. As much of the Australian withdrawal was executed under the cover of darkness, the signal wire also acted as a guide to keep the soldiers from losing the track.

Martin explained how the surgeon used the rock to perform amputations before the native carriers, affectionately referred to as Fuzzy Wuzzy Angels, carried the seriously wounded over eighty kilometres of mountains to reach the hospital in Port Moresby.

It took eight Fuzzy Wuzzies to carry one man all the way, so any Australian able to walk, did so to free up men to carry supplies to the troops still fighting.

---

[25] I'd become quite attached to my hiking poles despite of them feeling awkward on the first day.
[26] Butch was shot while handing out grenades to his unit in the heat of battle.
[27] Stan Bisset was an intelligence officer and survived the war. He died in 2010.

One soldier, shot in both ankles, crawled on his hands and knees for days so he wouldn't take the stretcher bearers away from someone who needed it more than him[28].

Matt asked about POWs on the track and Martin replied that there weren't any[29] due to the remote inhospitable conditions and lack of supplies. Also the Japanese believed surrendering was worse than death. The Australians quickly learned that any wounded left behind wouldn't be taken prisoner, but instead be tortured and killed.[30]

Martin pulled out a music docking station and the lyrics to *'Danny Boy'*. Butch and Stan had been great singers and Stan had reportedly sung *'Danny Boy'* to his brother as he lay dying in his arms. Martin hit play and we sang along to the song. Several of us had to wipe a stray tear away by the time we finished.

We headed back up to the track and kept walking. The PNG man who had been standing by the trekker fee sign, travelled with our group for the next few days.

It took another hour of undulating track to reach the village of Alola where we were meant to camp the previous night. We sat down on the grass while our trekking crew traded for supplies with the villagers.

Felicity's father, Anthony, sat down beside me. The three bandaids that he had on his legs when we met at the airport had multiplied.

"Did you slip?" I pointed to the mud on the back of his shorts. He nodded.

---

[28] He was later captured and killed by the Japanese, but received a medal for his actions.

[29] At some point during the campaign, prisoners were taken, but that may have been after the battle had left the Kokoda Track. Dugald Moyes, my grandad, learned to speak Japanese from a prisoner.

[30] The first prisoner Dugald Moyes interrogated died. We never found out any other details, but the event left Grandad shaken, even decades after the war. One story we were told, was that Grandad would offer the Japanese soldier half a cigarette. He'd get the other half after he talked. The prisoners were then handed over to some of the natives who still practiced cannibalism against their enemies.

"I fell over five times yesterday," he said.

I nodded. I'd only slipped once so far, but it was easy to do on the muddy track.

I took the opportunity to remove my boots and let my feet air. I had a hard blister on the side of one big toe, a blister under the nail of my second toe, and both my little toes were red and swollen. I pulled the bandaids and sports tape out of my bag and covered all the blisters and tender stops on my feet, leaving my footwear off until we were about to leave.

It took another hour-ish of downhill hiking before we reached a large creek crossing. A beautiful jungle-made bridge of saplings, vine, and occasional strand of wine, arched over the water. Ben took my hiking poles so I had both hands to use on the wide bridge.

Next was more uphill climbing. The mountain range went on and on, with an occasional downhill section before more uphill. At one point we climbed up the wet rocks of a cascade before the track appeared again. I spent all my time focused on my feet and wondering how anyone managed to fight on this track.

The Australians carried out a fighting withdrawal through this jungle and much of the falling back to fresh positions was done in the dark. Often small groups would get lost and some took days of struggling through the jungle to reach the retreating Australian position on the track. I was in awe of these men, as I struggled to keep my footing in the daylight with Ben to guide me.

I tried to work out how I would describe this track to someone. The best I could come up with was to imagine walking through a national park after heavy rain had made the track slippery. Now locate a narrow animal track travelling up or down the steepest section of terrain and follow it. If there is a 'Danger – Keep Out' sign, it's probably close to what we were experiencing.

The track steepened and Ben would reach down to haul me up by an arm to the next slick foothold. The angle of the track was such that on several occasions I bumped my head on the bottom of Ben's pack as he pulled me up.

At one point when we paused for a brief water break and I rested my fatiguing limbs, I checked the Garmin tied to my boot. It had a full red line indicating I'd been still too long and need to start moving. I cursed it and promised to write a strongly worded product review when I made it back to civilisation.

Shortly before midday, we made another stop. This time we left our porters and packs on the track, while one of the trekking crew and Martin lead us along a side trail. We took our hiking poles with us and stepped carefully in the knowledge that our porters were not with us to catch us when[31] we slipped.

After a short trek through the jungle, we crossed what appeared to be a dry creek bed[32], before scrambling up the other side and coming across a WWII Japanese dugout under and in between roots under a tree. It appeared to go back in a fair distance, but the spider webs around the entrance stopped me crawling into the hole to check.

We continued over to a small flat area under the jungle canopy. There was a protected view of the adjacent mountain ridge from where I could see a blue tarp over a hut in a distant clearing.

This was a Japanese mountain gun position. The enemy soldiers reportedly carried the guns over the track, each responsible for a different part that would then be assembled

---

[31] Rachael was the only one in our group who didn't slip during the ten day trek, although she did take a tumble off an unlevel step at one of the dining huts.

[32] The gravelly strip was bare of the usual dense jungle. On my return to Australia, I came across a book called '*The Lost Battlefield of Kokoda*' by Brian Freeman. It revealed that the Japanese had attempted to build a two metre wide road across the mountains so their horses and mules could haul their heavy mountain guns into position. What we had unknowingly walked across was a section of 'Jap Road'.

in location. This position[33], with an excellent view of anyone coming over the track on the other ridge, caused a lot of damage to the Australian advance until they eventually managed to capture the gun.

A small display of wartime relics, including a pair of grenades and mortar gun parts, lay among the tree roots. Someone had placed laminated information sheets to a couple of the trees regarding the weapons. We took photos so we could read the information later and headed back to our trekking crew.

The main track descended sharply to Eora Creek where another cleared campsite waited for our lunch stop. I removed my muddy gaiters, boots, and socks and walked around barefoot to give my blisters a rest, while lunch was prepared.

The dining hut jutted out over the bank of the river. It had a raised floor and half-height walls made of thick sheets of bark and we could see the river pebbles below our feet through the gaps in the floor.

Lunch was another pot of 2-minute noodles and a platter of sliced cheese, spam, and jungle-made scones. Anthony didn't touch any of the food, preferring to eat his stash of muesli bars. It started to drizzle while we ate and we rushed out to retrieve our bags and boots sitting out on the grass.

While everyone was present, I shared a hand-drawn sketch of the PNG coast to the north-west of our location. The Japanese characters marked locations as well as where enemy (Allied) troops had been sighted.

---

[33] '*The Lost Battlefield of Kokoda*' book also revealed that this was not the main Japanese position as previously thought. Five hundred metres higher up the mountain ridge (around two hours hike – in trekker time) is the main site, reported to be completely intact, bullets lying where they fell, untouched for 75 years. The site is on the traditional hunting land of Alola Village, and at the time of writing, not open to trekkers. The site needs to be properly protected first and decisions to be made regarding the recovery of the Australian and Japanese remains.

Another trekking group came down the ridge and as we occupied the hut, they kept walking. We followed not long afterwards, the track winding along the edge of the river until we reached another beautifully constructed jungle bridge.

We crossed the creek and climbed back up the other side of the ridge before arriving at the cleared campsite with the blue tarp we had seen from the mountain gun position. The Japanese location was completely obscured by the jungle and even when Vicko pointed out the general direction, I couldn't make out the place.

A plaque sat alone in the clearing:

> 1942   Eora Creek   1992
>
> The Eora Creek crossing represented one of the best defensive positions on the Kokoda Trail between Port Moresby and Kokoda. On 1 September 1942 it was successfully defended from its east bank for 2 days by the retreating Australians who were against a much larger Japanese force. Constant rain, the deep ravine and swirling Eora Creek with limited log crossings made the area a nightmare in which to fight.
>
> The Japanese made the whole area a major defensive position during their retreat. The tired Japanese resisted determined frontal attacks by fresh Australian troops from 22 October for over a week. Australians advancing on the west bank of Eora Creek overcame the enemy eventually and when almost encircled, the Japanese hastily abandoned their positions retreating to Oivi and Gorari.
>
> Eora Creek Village once in the centre of much of the heavy fighting, now lies abandoned. The crashing, haunting noise of the fast flowing creek below brings vividly to mind the turmoil of battle, and the men who fought here so long ago.

The trekking group, who passed us during lunch, sat around on the ground, each with a little bag of food and waiting for their 2-minute noodles to cook in their bowl of hot water. It made us feel like we had the 5-star trekking option with our meals prepared for us.

Just past where they sat, we were confronted with the start of what seemed like a never-ending mountain. We climbed for a while and then would rest at what appeared to be the peak, only every time we started walking again, the track continued to wind upwards.

"Is this this top?" Andrew asked as we waited for the others. Vicko shook his head.

"I read that one of these mountains has a heap of false peaks," I said.

"This one," Vicko replied, nodding.

We continued on. As we were having a water break at another of the peaks, one of our trekking crew strode past with a full pack on his back and another slung under one arm.

We found out later that Anthony had slipped again, landing on his back on a tree root. He took two codeine tablets, but was still in pain and struggling to walk.

His porter plus another had passed their packs onto two other boys, so they were free to help Anthony make it to our campsite for the night.

My calves and thighs burned by the time we reached the actual peak of the mountain. We almost didn't believe it was the top when Vicko told us, as we were surrounded by jungle canopy and higher ridges off to the side of the track, but after our break we started the descent towards our campsite.

I became less focused after so many hours walking. The steep downhill sections were hard on my knees and at times we had to climb over big fallen tree trunks while the narrow, slippery track hugged the mountain ridge.

Later that afternoon, we reached Templeton's Crossing 2. The first campsite was already occupied by a trekking group. We kept walking, passing another war history plaque:

1942   Templeton's Crossing   1992

The location of the crossing of Eora Creek has varied over the years. The area which is now overgrown, was a major Australian supply depot during the Kokoda Campaign. The crossing was named after an Australian officer killed at Oivi on 26 July 1942.

On 3 September 1942 the Japanese captured Templeton's Crossing while in close pursuit of the Australians. From here the Australians fell back steadily. They abandoned the air dropping zone at Myola and only found a secure defensive position at Brigade Hill just south of Efogi. Later as the Japanese retreated they made their first major stand against the advancing Australians here at Templeton's Crossing. On 12 October the Australians attacked from the south and west but took 4 days to dislodge the enemy. Ahead lay Eora Creek which took the Australians a further 13 days to capture though only 3 hours walking distance.

All wounded faced a daunting trek to reach major medical facilities. As there was no air evacuation the wounded struggled along the muddy trail for seemingly endless days. Many would have perished, had it not been for the enduring and loyal native stretcher bearers.

We crossed the roaring river with the help of a narrow plank bridge and single rope to hold onto. Ben walked close behind me with a hand on the back of my bag until I reached the safety of the other side.

The boys pitched our tents on the cleared ground by the noisy river. We washed our clothes in the cold water, but it started to drizzle again in the evening and they didn't fully dry.

The group we passed earlier arrived and set up camp on our side of the river in the next clearing. They had their own dining hut and toilets, so we didn't need to share.

Our toilet was another little hut with a hole in the ground. The timber planks were widely spaced and I worried about falling in or dropping my torch in the dark, but I managed without incident.

The ground between the hut, toilet, and tents was slippery with mud and I was tempted to use my walking poles to get around camp. After only two days, it felt strange to walk without them.

Anthony was still in pain, but wanted to see how he felt in the morning before making a decision to continue the trek or be evacuated. Felicity was torn between continuing the trek or leaving with her father. We didn't see a lot of Martin as he went straight to his tent to rest.

My camera battery started to flash empty and I worried my spare wouldn't last until the end of the trek. We still had another week ahead of us and my first battery had only lasted three days.

We had a late jungle bedtime of 8pm. Garmin said I'd done 18,698 steps, but I'd stopped believing it. I recorded the number anyway for the sake of consistency.

The temperate dropped quickly so I donned my thermal underwear and wrapped myself in my sleeping bag. I fell sleep, only to wake at 2:30 am to the sound of rain drowning out the roar of the river. It almost sounded pleasant until I thought about how slippery it would make the track in the morning.

At least I had a different tent to the one from the first night so I stayed dry and eventually drifted back to sleep.

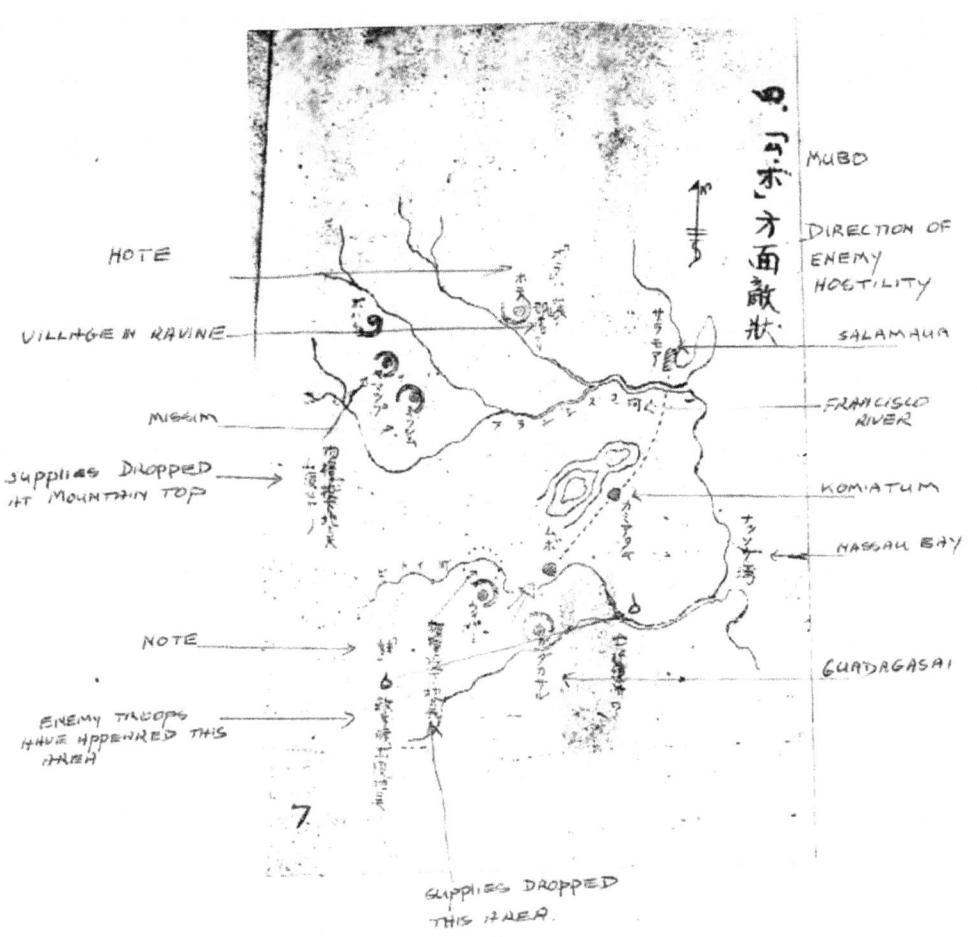

WWII Japanese sketch of Salamaua area. This is to the north-west of Kokoda.

Above: A collection of WWII artefacts displayed by the plaque dedicated to Butch and Stan Bisset.

Left: Conn's Rock. The Australian army surgeon used the relatively flat rock to perform surgeries and amputations before the wounded were carried back over the track towards the hospital at Port Moresby. The local landowners decorate the rock with flowers and leaves.

Left: Looking down off the track at the next creek to be crossed. It was a steep scramble down to reach it.

Below: A small waterfall beside the track.

Left: Approaching Alola Village.

Right: View from the Japanese mountain gun position

Below: Looking back the way we came. It was a steep climb to reach this rest stop at the crest in the track.

Above: A jungle-made bridge.

Below: Eora Creek.

Day 4 – Templeton's Crossing to Naduri
20th April 2017

Mist had settled over our camp when we rose in the morning. Martin hiked up the track to find reception for the satellite phone to call the helicopter for Anthony. Felicity was still undecided if she'd stay with us or leave with her father.

After breakfast we said goodbye to Anthony, as well as Felicity in case she didn't re-join the group. Martin stayed behind with the sat-phone and their porters to wait for the helicopter.

The group who camped beside us last night set off up the track, and we followed behind shortly after. We crossed back over the narrow plank bridge spanning the rushing river, before turning uphill.

We climbed for half an hour before stopping to rest while the tail end of the group caught up. Rocks and tree roots interspersed the muddy track and we pondered if we could change the game of *'rock, paper, scissors'* to *'mud, rock, tree-root'*. We got stuck when we realised the mud trumped everything else due to its slipperiness.

The next half hour was steeper still and my short legs slowed the group down. At one point while I was trying to work out how to reach the next step without my pack toppling me backwards, Matt called up jokingly from below to ask if I'd stopped to take a photo.

Vicko stopped suddenly and pointed to the ground. I peered around him in time to see a small brown snake slither across the track in front of us before disappearing into the jungle.

"Is it venomous?" I asked.

"No." Vicko shook his head. "Not the ones in the mountains. Only the ones down by the coast."

The cloud sat low over the mountains all day, so after stopping for five minutes, we'd grow cold and despite having tired legs, we begged Vicko to keep going so we could warm up again. Unfortunately for the slower part of the group, this reduced their rest time. With less recovery, they slowed down even further.

While we were stopped, the sound of the helicopter reached us through the jungle canopy. We paused for a moment, knowing our team mates[34] were on their way back to Port Moresby, and Martin was an hour behind us.

When it began to drizzle, we paused to pull the waterproof covers over our packs. The track wound upwards again and after finally dragging ourselves over the peak, we sat down to rest on an old mossy fallen tree trunk.

As we sat there drinking water and recuperating from the climb, a bare-foot five year old girl[35], carrying just a Coke bottle filled with water, wandered up the hill.

She paused when she saw us, as though wondering why we had chosen to sit down at the top of this hill, but Vicko waved her on down the track.

"Well, that doesn't make me feel insecure about my trekking ability," I muttered.

Vicko led us down the same path and we were immediately faced with another steep downhill section. My left knee started to twinge at the back like it does after a dislocation. I've dislocated my knees on several occasions since the age of eighteen. It wasn't something I wanted to do on the track.

Grandad always hated walking downhill. My sister and I couldn't understand it as we felt it was easier than uphill. On this hill, as I took each careful step on the slippy descent, I finally understood his point of view. My knees protested with each steep step.

Danni who had short legs like me, resorted to sitting down on some of the foot holds to reach the next one. Despite her

---

[34] Felicity decided to remain with her injured father. She will attempt the track again at a later date.
[35] We were told she was the niece of one of our trekking crew.

muddy behind, I was tempted do the same to get down the mountainside.

The terrain eventually levelled out and although it was easier on the knees, water sat on the track so we trudged through sloppy mud that made walking feel more like skating on ice. In some locations, tree branches lay along the track and we walked across them to stay above the mud.

"It's like the swamp from *Star Wars*," Andrew said from somewhere behind me.

"I was thinking the scene from *Lord of the Rings*," Rachael replied.

"Really? I was picturing the swamp from *Princess Bride* and hoping there were no Rodents of Unusual Size hiding in the undergrowth," I added as I followed Ben's footsteps.

I paused occasionally to take a photo and my first camera card filled up, shortly followed by the battery going flat. We still had six days left on the track, so I put my spares in and started rationing my photo taking.

We picked our way down another hill as the sound of rushing water grew closer. When we reached the river we'd been hearing, there was another jungle-made bridge. We crossed it and climbed up the other side to Templeton's Crossing 1 campsite.

We had our break in the dining hut, eating our trekking snacks while watching chickens[36] roam the grassy area nearby.

The track ahead of us wound upwards once more, reaching towards the highest point of the trek. The challenging terrain meant it took a long time to travel what would otherwise be a reasonably short distance.

During WWII, the commanders in Port Moresby blamed the officers on the ground for the troop movements being so slow. They never sighted the track to see why. Travel is

---

[36] Each chicken had a ribbon tied to a wing feather and we assumed it was to identify it as belonging to a particular family.

measured by time rather than distance across the mountain range.

As lunch time approached, we stopped at a large flat campsite called 1900 Crossing. My knees made it painful to walk and I hobbled carefully over to the dining hut. My pants wouldn't roll up high enough for me to tape my knees, so I borrowed Matthew's shawl[37] to wrap around my waist and removed my pants. Luckily I brought a whole roll of sports tape and had checked how to strap a knee before the trek.

I managed to get the tape and my stretchy pants back on, before I realised I needed the toilet. The little hut was a slippery hike back up to the edge of the clearing. The toilet was another hole in the ground and with well-taped knees, it was difficult to squat. I made it back to the dining hut with the aid of my hiking poles.

A narrow stream separated us from another part of the cleared campsite. The group who had been travelling slightly ahead of us were in the hut on the other side. They headed off before we finished our lunch of 2-minute noodles.

The clearing around the dining hut and the track further on were surrounded by pandanus[38] trees with their roots beginning well above the ground so they looked like upright straw brooms.

While we ate lunch, I pulled out another WWII Japanese document from my bag and read out Grandad's translation:

> Read this alone – and the war can be won.
> 1. Campaign area in South Asia – what it is like
> - A treasure house of the Far East seized by the British, Americans, French, Dutch
> - A hundred million Asians tyrannized by three hundred thousand whites
> - A world source of oil, rubber, tin

---

[37] He'd been using it as a sweat rag.
[38] These trees have many uses including the leaves being used to make the roofs on the huts we encountered at each village and campsite.

- A world of everlasting sunshine/summer
2. Why must we fight. How should we fight.
- Obeying the Emperor's August wish for peace in the Far East
- You may be killed in battle, but don't die of disease
3. From the long voyage to the landing assault
4. What are you to do on the ship
5. The landing assault
6. Marching through the tropics
7. Camp in the tropics

We Japanese have been born in a country of no mean blessings and thanks to the August favour and influence of his Majesty the Emperor, our land has never once to this day experienced invasion and occupation by a foreign power. The other peoples of the Far East look with envy upon Japan, they trust and honour the Japanese and deep in their hearts they are hoping that with the help of the Japanese people they may themselves achieve natural independence and happiness.

Officers and men, the eyes of the whole world will be upon you in this campaign and working together in community of spirit, you must demonstrate to the world the true value of Japanese manhood. His Imperial Majesty's desire for peace in the Far East and to set Asia free rests equally on our shoulders.

"I think the dot points are topics for discussion," I said.

"Sounds like some meetings I've been to," Andrew joked as I tucked the paper back into my pack.

After lunch, the track was less steep[39], but very muddy. We joked about Rachael getting a spot of mud on her legs while

---

[39] Still steep, but not steep-steep, or ridiculously steep. It's a mountain range – most of it is some degree of 'steep'.

the rest of us were covered in the stuff up to our knees. We were baffled by how she had remained clean up until that point.

The helicopter flew over the track again. *"Hunger Games,"* Nicole whispered, while we wondered who was being evacuated.

At some point the track split into two routes. One headed past Myola 1, a large flat site used for dumping supplies by plane in 1942. We didn't take that route as we travelled too slowly through the mud and needed to make camp before dark. I was busy watching my feet so I missed seeing the turn-off, following blindly after Vicko and Ben.

Vicko stopped us just before the track descended sharply again. I looked past him to where it split into two parallel routes from people trying to find the best way up or down the slippery track. Neither option looked great to me – it was all mud, without the rocks or tree roots for purchase. The clouds pressed in around us obscuring the view and giving a misty vibe to the whole scene.

"Now for some fun," Vicko said when the whole group had gathered. He set off down the left hand side of the track. Ben followed closely behind me, his hand on the back of my bag, as I moved after Vicko.

"What this track needs is a zip-line," I said, glancing at the track disappearing into the jungle below us.

We hadn't gone far before Vicko called out, "Road block!"

The narrow track ahead was obstructed by fallen trees. Some had been down long enough for someone to cut a notch onto the wood as a flat step on top of the fallen trunk.

The sports tape on my knees offered support and reduced the pain, but limited my range of movement. Ben walked in front of me, giving me a hand down from the bigger tree trunks.

A couple of trunks we ducked under, and Ben's full pack scrapped the bark as he squeezed himself through the gap. I was glad for my small pack and wondered how Ron, Matt and Andrew were managing with their big packs.

The front half of our group had made it through the long obstacle course and onto flatter ground when we heard a shriek behind us[40]. Vicko paused, but there were no further calls so we moved on again.

Not long after, a sound like a gunshot echoed through the jungle, but under the canopy it was difficult to tell where it originated or from how far away. I thought it came from behind us. Vicko glanced around at the dense jungle, but kept walking. My thoughts went briefly to the men who fought on this track seventy-five years ago.

A few steps further on and three more shots rang out, followed moments later by loud crackling like firecrackers going off. Finally, the unmistakable sound of a massive tree crashing through the undergrowth sounded behind us where the tail end of our group still was. We stopped and looked behind us in concern.

As soon as the jungle was quite again, Vicko and the boys called out in their native language. The boys further up the track responded in kind. Satisfied no one was injured, we continued on. The massive tree had fallen downhill - away from the track, although it had been uncomfortably close to the back of our group.

---

[40] Danni had slipped on the track and landed on top of Danny - her porter - as he tried to catch her.

We ended our day with another long descent. By the map we were doing half of it that afternoon and the other half the next morning after we broke camp.

Ben held tightly to the back of my bag as I placed each foot carefully. At one point, Ben was the one to slip, kicking mud up the backs of my legs as his feet slid out from under him. He bounded straight back up again to keep me on my feet.

I was thankful I'd strapped my knees. Although they ached, they held up under the strain of the descent.

Muddy water flowed down a series of slippery steps made from the trekkers who had passed before us.

"The mud is going faster than me," Matthew muttered behind me.

The jungle thinned as we neared the next village. A long fence made of branches and small trees ran along the side of the track, protecting sweet potato crops. Huts could be seen through the clouds several rolling hills away.

We slid across the ground until Vicko stopped us just up from the village to wait for the rest of the group. Matt jogged up a short hill to get a photo with some kids playing ball on the plateau above us. There was no way I could have made it up there with him. My exhausted legs trembled and I shifted from one foot to the other while we waited. I wanted to sit down, but the ground was too wet and I might not have been able to get up again if I sat.

Carla, Danni, and Nicole arrived with their porters and Vicko led us into Naduri Village as a group. The village was notably wealthier than the others we had passed. One large building sat on concrete stumps and had corrugated iron walls and roof with a solar hot water tank perched on top.

A large sign on the roof proclaimed, "Australian AID. The Governments of Papua New Guinea and Australia proudly supporting better health along the Kokoda Track."

Tables made of branches lined the track to the village campsite. Women hovered by their stalls of hand-made 'bilum' bags, soft drinks, and Twisties.

A group of children stood under a hand-made sign that said, 'Welcome to Naduri Village, Back Track Adventure trekkers. God blessed you all. Welcome welcome welcome.'

They sung us songs to welcome us into the village and they came forward to put flower leis around our necks. It was a lovely welcome, but all I really wanted was to get off my feet and remove my boots. I leant on my poles trying to take as much weight as I could off my aching legs. When the children finished their welcome, we made our way past them, shaking their hands as we went, to the cleared grassy area where we would camp.

Several of our trekking crew were from this village, so after our tents were set up, they disappeared to spent time with their families.

We took our boots and gaiters to the shower and washed our legs and gear under the cold water. It took some time to clean up as the water stopped every time the pressure dropped – probably due to the other trekking group camped at another site within shouting distance of ours.

Dusk settled not long after we finished and we sat around a camp fire set on the dirt floor of an open hut. Ron borrowed a timber ladder to hang across the rafters for us to dry our clothes, but by the end of the night they were more smoky than dry.

A camp dog crept up to our fire to warm itself in the cool evening and Matthew told it to go away. It ignored him, lying down on the dirt before the flames.

"Maybe you have to speak Pidgin[41]," Andrew suggested.

"Coo, coo," Matthew said to the dog in an imitation of a pidgin as he flapped his arms. The dog crept away under the hut only to come back later to sit by the fire.

Martin made it into camp and collapsed in his tent. Carla spent the evening monitoring his deteriorating condition. She had left her thermometer and thermal blanket back in Port Moresby thinking she was over-packing.

After dinner, the village leader Joel joined us in the dining hut to welcome us to his home. The children filed in to sing to us. Some songs involved our participation, such as one where we all introduced ourselves; *'My name is Nikki and I love the Lord. My name is Nikki and I love you all'*.[42] We took it in turns singing our names while I wondered if anyone in our group was actually religious.

It was getting late and we were exhausted from trekking all day. Joel told us the kids would sing one final song. We breathed a sigh of relief imagining our beds, even though we've enjoyed the interaction with the villagers.

Joel gave us a brief warning that we'd be singing the Australian Anthem next and I tried to remember the whole verse while we all stood and the kids sang the PNG Anthem. When it was our turn, we got through the song without too many stumbles despite it being a long time since any of us had sung it. Nicole even knew the second verse.

---

[41] Pidgin English is the main language spoken in PNG.
[42] The villagers were Seventh Day Adventist so many of the songs involved praising Jesus.

The kids gave us a couple more 'final' songs before a farewell song. They passed us in a line, shaking our hands as they sang and gave us bouquets of flowers made from the local jungle plants. I ended up with two. One began to fall apart in my hands so I left it in the hut, taking the other one with me.

It was 10pm by the time we crawled into our tents. My Garmin only recorded 19,920 steps for the day.

Right: Parts of the track were reduced to slippery mud grooves and it was difficult to keep your footing.

Left: Templeton's Crossing 2 surrounded by early morning mist.

Above: Mist settled over a rest stop.

Left: Vicko waits for the whole group to catch up.

Right: The slippery track splits in two before dropping away into a 'road block'.

Left: More slippery mud track winding through the mist.

Below: Approaching Naduri Village past the fence separating the track from the village crops.

Day 5 – Naduri to Menari
21st April 2017

I woke at 4:55 am to an actual rooster crowing, although the others claimed he'd been crowing for at least an hour before I heard him.

Carla's wake up call sounded like a chicken laying an egg. She hadn't had any sleep, staying in Martin's tent all night to keep an eye on his fluctuating temperature.

While we had breakfast, she tried to get reception on the satellite phone so Martin could be evacuated back to Port Moresby. She had no luck, so the boys used the radio system between villages to get hold of the helicopter pilot.

While that was going on, village leader Joel gave us a talk about the history of his land, often speaking quickly in what appeared to be a prepared speech brought out for passing Australian trekkers.

"You as Australians wouldn't be here without the aid of the Fuzzy Wuzzy Angels during the war, and our people wouldn't be here without the sacrifice of your grandfathers," Joel said.

As he spoke, I thought of Grandad here as an eighteen year old boy, and it left me with a deep feeling of connection to these people and their land.

Joel showed us into a hut protecting the grave of Naduri's last Fuzzy Wuzzy Angel who helped our soldiers in 1942. Ovuru Indiki passed away in 2013 and his grave was surrounded by bright faux flowers. Joel led us in a minute silence.

"Lest we forget," we murmured at the conclusion. There were a few teary eyes as we paid our respects to those who defended us during WWII.

Outside, Joel gave us some history of the PNG people. They used to be separate warring tribes, some even practiced cannabilism. He pointed out the frame of a hut on stilts on display at the top of the rise above our campsite. The men would build huts on stilts with a ladder to reach them, so they could defend their women and children from raiding parties.

"You can see the villages are no longer at war with each other because our huts are built on the ground now," Joel said.

The cooking fires we'd seen built on dirt floors obviously wouldn't be a good idea in a raised hut. So the fire didn't burn through the wooden floor, rocks were laid over leaves. Soil was piled on top before a fire could be lit.

"You tell all your family and friends about the welcome you received here," Joel said.

We set off at 7:30 am after Joel had finished his history. Most of us had flower bouquets tucked into our bags and leis around our necks. We left Martin behind with the villagers and sat-phone to wait for the helicopter. We found out later, that when he reached Port Moresby Hospital, Martin was diagnosed with typhoid. He was sent back to Australia before we made it back to Port Moresby. We had now lost three of our original group of thirteen Australian trekkers.

We descended along the track until we came to a bridge made of small tree trunks tied together and balanced across two large boulders in the white-water creek. A rope was already strung out between the banks to hold on to.

Another trekking group, heading in the opposite direction to us, reached the bridge first and we had a rest break while they crossed.

After our turn, we headed up the next mountain ridge. The track was rocky, and between the rocks and the tree roots, our feet had something to brace against in the mud. Creeks cut across the track and sometimes we walked up the wet rocks before the path veered away from the water again.

We came out at the peak marked on our map as Efogi 2. The village map and radio point called the place Launumu Village. Ron discovered USB charging ports at the radio point and took the opportunity to charge his devices while we rested in the dining hut. Unfortunately, my camera didn't have a USB port so I couldn't charge my batteries.

A few huts in the village had corrugated iron roofs, althought the walls were the traditional woven style.

A market stall was set up beside the track selling hand-made bilum bags and fruit. We bought a bunch of bananas for energy to reach our lunch stop and a couple of avocados to eat with lunch. The avocados were round and the size of a small melon.

Our rest break felt long, but the rear of the group didn't get much time before we kept moving. Last night, Carla told us we only had five hours walking today, but looking at our map, we realised her information was incorrect[43]. My map's estimate was seven hours, but we were still travelling slower than the estimates due to the wet conditions[44].

It took over an hour to hike downhill to reach Efogi Village[45], where to our delight there was a sign stating, *'Kokoda 48.1 km, Owers Cnr 45.5 kms'*. We'd passed the halfway point, although we still had another four hours walking to reach camp and it was 11:30 am already.

Efogi village was large and sprawling, with the standard neatly mown grass and levelled dirt under the huts. One building even claimed to be a guest house where trekkers could pay to stay the night.

At the village market, I saw a small blue wool bilum bag with the PNG flag and *'Kokoda Track 75th Anniversary'* woven into it. I bought it for eighty kina[46].

"Excuse me, you forgot your sticks," the woman called out as I walked off. She pointed to the hiking poles I'd left jammed into the ground beside her table.

"Thanks, I won't get far without those," I said, jogging back to grab them.

We stopped for lunch (same menu as every other day, but with one of the avacados we bought at the last village) a short distance from the market stalls.

---

[43] This was Carla's second time on the track and the first time she had trekked in the other direction, so it was all fairly new to her and she relied on information given to her by others.

[44] April is apparently one of the most difficult times to tackle the trek.

[45] Marked on the map as Efogi 1.

[46] I also bought my first soft drink for the trek, many villages along the track sold them for seven kina each to thirsty trekkers.

Matthew discovered he left his shawl at the last village. One of the boys jogged back to fetch it. He arrived back with the missing shawl long before we left the village, despite the fact it took us over an hour to walk the distance one way.

Efogi had a village museum with a five kina fee to enter the small hut. Inside was a sword in a case that had been presented to Efogi Village in recognition of the support provided to the Australian Defence Force during the Kokoda Campaign of July-November 1942. A collection of rusted helmets and weapon parts lined the shelves, and a table of shoe fragmets still contained the toe bones of their owners.

I pulled out my favourite document from Grandad's paperwork - the Japanese Firing Sketch for the north side of Efogi, dated 7th September 1942. It had the enemy (Australian) positions marked and the Japanese light and heavy machine guns lining up those positions. I passed it around the group before leaving it behind for the Efogi Museum.

I never quite worked out the exact position of the firing sketch as Martin was our history guru, but I believe the battle occurred further up the next ridge from the current village.

With Matthew's shawl back[47] we put our boots back on and shouldered our packs. On the south side of the village was the ranger station and our trekking crew lined up to have their bags weighed on a set of scales and hook.

"How much are they allowed to carry?" I asked.

"Twenty kilograms," Vicko replied.[48]

We watched as several of the boys removed items from their packs to be re-distributed among the others under the weight limit. One of the boys had 27 kgs in his pack. Rachael's porter was only carrying 15 kg. Our three guys with full packs weighed their bags out of interest. Andrew's was the lightest at 13 kg, but Matt was carrying 17kg.

---

[47] He's insisted it was needed it case I had to remove my pants again and referred to it as Nikki's privacy shawl from then on.

[48] One of the porters claimed it was 25 kg, but I'm not sure which figure was correct.

Outside the village, the track headed up along the edge of the mountain. In some places the single file trail had become sloped and the only thing preventing our feet sliding off the edge was a small mound of accumulated mud from the feet of those who passed before us. Our porters walked close behind us, ready to grab our packs if we stumbled.

We reached a short, but steep and narrow section of track with a fence separating us from the vertical drop. The fence made me nervous as we'd been walking along the edge of drop-offs for a while now, but someone considered this one dangerous enough to require a barrier. I leaned in towards the mountainside and breathed a sigh of relief once we'd passed.

Further on, a hand-painted sign marked the Brigade Hill site fee collection point. Once again, the ten kina had already been arranged by Stanley and we kept climbing up over the ridge.

We emerged onto the grassy ridge of Brigade Hill. Rows of white sticks protuding from the ground marked the Australians who died here in 1942. A couple of the trekking crew got here before us and set up the PNG and Australian flags from tall saplings that they wedged into the ground as flag poles either side of the memerial plaques.

Brigade Hill
6-9 September 1942

This hill over which you walk was the site where one thousand Australians temporarily held back a much larger Japanese force advancing towards Port Moresby. In bitter fighting many men of both sides died. Today only their dust and memories of their sacrifices remain.

This area has been preserved by the Koiari people and to them we all extend our gratitude for their thoughtfulness and kindness.

Brigade Hill Memorial

In honour of Capt. Claude Nye and the brave men of $2/14^{th}$, $2/16^{th}$, $2/27^{th}$ Battalions & 21 Brig. H.O. A.I.F.

Grandad's Japanese firing sketch was dated 7th September – right in the middle of the dates listed on the Bridge Hill plaque.

Before coming on the trek, I finished reading a book called, *'The Bone Man of Kokoda'* by Charles Happell about the sole surviver of a Japanese unit who attacked the Australians in this location. They attacked from up the side of the mountain while other units came up the track. I peered over the edge of the ridge. The terrain was ridiculously steep and it would have been difficult enough to climb unburdened, but they did it while carrying weapons.

Our group gathered around the memorial on the ridge where the boys had raised the Australian and PNG flags. We held a little ceremony for those who died on that hill and Carla pulled out Martin's music dock to play the *Last Post*. We didn't have a wreath to lay so I removed the bouquet of flowers[49] from a loop on my bag and left it beside the other offerings at the base of the plaque.

Matt pulled out the map which showed we had more than two and a half hours to reach the village we'd be camping at. Worried we won't make it before dark, he took the lead behind Vicko when we set off. Rachael followed him and they disappeared into the jungle.

I walked with Ben and Andrew, occasionally glancing behind me to made sure Andrew was still with me and my porter, so he was not alone in the jungle. He kept up with us easily.

I didn't see Matt and Rachael until we stopped for a break, and we started walking again as soon as we saw the tail end of our group approach. Everyone apart from the slow group went ahead of me, disappearing out of sight within minutes.

Ben walked behind me and as I had no footsteps to follow, I didn't know where was the best place to step. I had to slow down, looking up regularly to pick my way along the track.

I found myself becoming annoyed that the others left me behind. It was weird, because I normally liked bushwalking on

---

[49] The flowers the children of Naduri Village had given me the night before.

my own. It gave me the sensation of being the only one to experience the view without being surrounded by others.

On this remote jungle track, it made me anxious. If I slipped and fell, Ben was the only one to help. There was only one satellite phone in the whole group and it had been left with Martin. I had no idea if it had made it back to the group after Martin was evacuated. If an accident happened, we'd have to rely on someone running to the closest village for assistance.

Tree roots intersected the track as we made our way downhill. It gave me something to stop my feet slipping with each step. Occasionally the track split into two options. If I paused, not knowing which option would be the least tricky, Ben pointed to one or the other and I took that direction.

Another trekking team passed us from the other direction. Ben and I stood among the tree roots beside the track to let them pass.

"How far is it?" one of them asked.

"Depends where you're stopping," I replied. It felt like we left Brigade Hill ages ago.

I caught up with our group at a rest stop. Our destination, Menari Village could be seen through a gap in the trees on the next ridge.

As soon as we started walking again, I lost the group. Matt joggged down the slippery slopes, where as I had to place each foot carefully so I didn't injure my knees.

The mountain seemed to go on forever. I stopped enjoying the present and instead focused on Saturday being a rest day. I just needed to make it to the next campsite.

Somewhere near the bottom, I overtook a middle-aged man being helped by two porters, one behind him and the other in front, guiding him down each step. The man looked exhausted, each step taking a monumental effort, and not too happy about being overtaken by a girl. The three of them stood to one side as Ben and I passed.

The track descended rapidly and a porter from a different trekking company jogged up the track. He paused to give me a hand down several narrow steps before continuing on his way, probably to assist the man behind me.

The ground dropped away revealing a rope strung out to assist trekkers down the cliff. I gripped it in one hand and both my hiking poles in the other. Ben held the rope in one hand and the back of my bag in the other. As I took each slow, careful step, I wondered how the porters were going to get the man I passed down this section.

At the bottom, a bridge spanned a large creek. The daylight was fading as I crossed, but I was sure the village would be just up the ridge a short way. I made it to the other side of the creek and stopped. The track vanished into the surrounding jungle. I was faced with the rocky bank of the creek, the jungle, and a cascade of water rushing down the rocks in front of me. As I'd lost my group, I had no idea where to go next.

Ben appeared behind me and pointed to the waterfall. I looked at him in disbelief, but that was definitely where he was directing me. I started forward again, picking my way up the wet rocks as the water flowed past me. After some time, the track appeared on my left and I had something to follow uphill again.

The track continued up a narrow route before widening into a slippery ascending grass path. It gave me hope that I was near the village, but it continued on and on as the light faded. I lengthened my stride as much as possible on the slippery grass. I'd still not seen the front or back of our group.

Finally the jungle opened out onto Menari Village. A trekking group camped on my left and a small airstrip stretched out on the right. I walked past the first camp and then another occupied site. I dragged my aching body the length of the airstrip before Ben finally pointed me to the right and then right again at a fork in the path.

At 6:15 pm, I finally made it into our camp. I'd been on the track for more than ten hours. I collapsed in the tent Ben pitched.

No one from the front of our group were waiting when I arrived or even checked on me which didn't improve my mood. I pulled my muddy boots off and cleaned up while keeping an ear out for the last of our group.

I stuck my head out of the tent when I heard people a short time later, but it was only trekking crew who had grabbed the tents from the porters still on the track so they'll be set up when the last of our group arrived. Just before dark, Adrian appeared. I called out to him so he knew someone noticed his arrival.

It was after dark when Danni, Nicole, and Carla arrived wearing their head torches. Our whole group had finally made it into camp. I made sure to greet them before making my way to the dining hut.

The others hadn't left us any prawn crackers, but dinner arrived shortly afterwards. We ate, worked out where the toilets were in the dark, and went to bed. My Garmin recorded 23,123 steps for the day.

Above: A log bridge crossing not far from Naduri Village

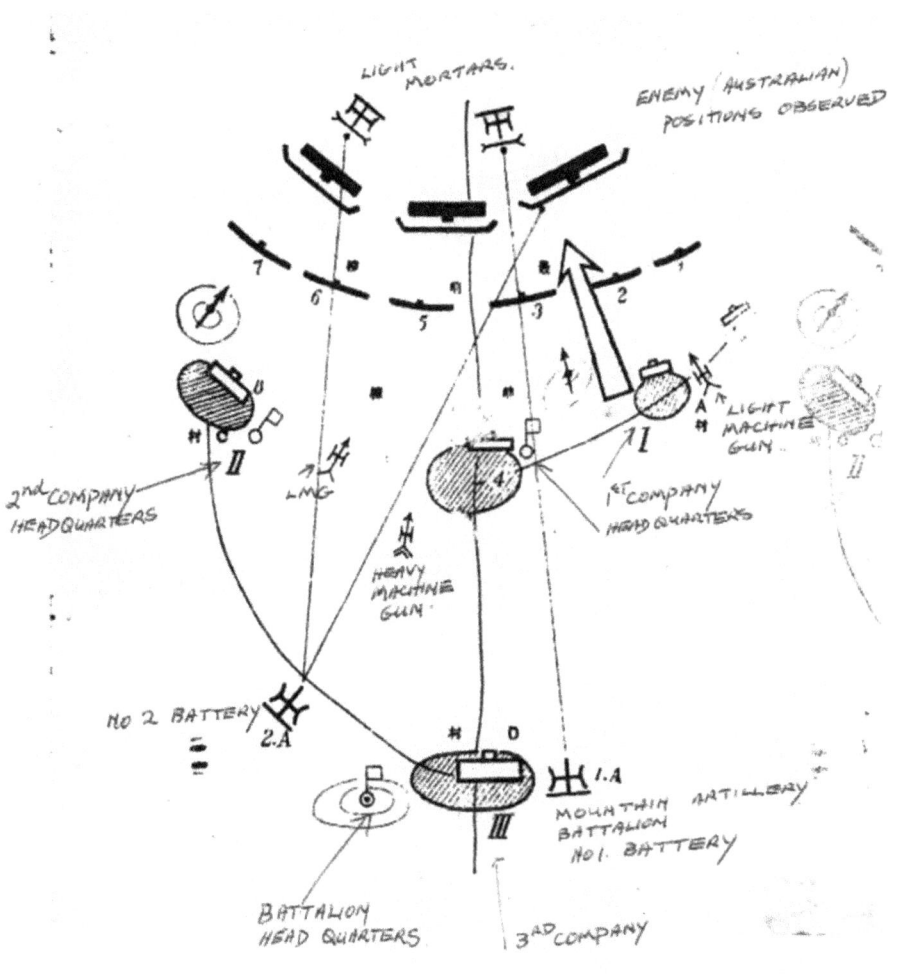

Japanese Firing Sketch document belonging to Dugald Moyes, Allied Translator and Interpreter Service, 1942.

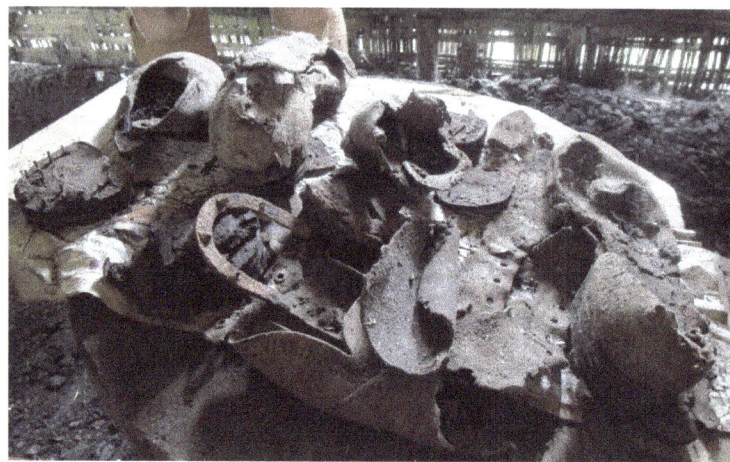

Top Left: The structure of a raised hut like the villagers used when they were at war with each other.

Top Right: WWII Japanese and Australian shoe fragments at Efogi Museum. Some of the shoes still contained toe bones.

Below: Looking back down the track towards the rear end of our group.

A log crossing. Vicko tied out the blue rope for us to use as a grab hold while crossing.

Left: Approaching Brigade Hill.

Below: Brigade Hill with sticks marking each Australian who died defending this hill in 1942.

Day 6 – The Sabbath
22nd April 2017

Voices coming from the campsite on the other side of the hedge woke me briefly around 4:30 am. I drifted back to sleep and woke a second time as the sun was rising.

Most of the villagers were Seventh Day Adventist, so Saturday was a no-work day. To respect their culture, we stopped trekking for the day[50]. The other three groups camped at Menari last night had continued on by the time we got up.

We ate a leisurely breakfast and washed our clothes under a nearby tap. The boys strung out the blue rope between some trees as a clothesline and it was soon full of drying clothing. I took the opportunity to point out that I had two identical blue shirts and hadn't actually been wearing the same shirt for the whole trek.

At 9:00 am, we followed the track through the village to the church. The building was made with the traditional timber frame and a corrugated iron roof. The walls were a mix of traditional weaving and corrugated iron.

We took seats on the back benches behind our porters who were all in clean clothes for the occasion. I'm not religious, but we were welcomed with open arms into the village.

The priest acknowledged us and our trekking crew. The villagers sang songs such as *'It's Not an Easy Road'*[51], and we were all invited to the front to introduce ourselves to the gathering. Our porters took a turn to sing one of their songs they had been practicing.

The helicopter could be heard over the singing. Carla had tried to be positive and mention it was used to carry supplies into the villages and that it wasn't always around due to

---

[50] Only three trekking companies currently stop trekking for the Sabbath and Back Track Adventures is one of those.

[51] This appeared to be a popular song for villagers to sing to us as we trekked over the mountain range.

evacuations. None of us thought they would do supply runs on the Sabbath though.

After the service we headed outside and checked out the village map point. We were well over halfway and had completed the highest peaks. The ridges ahead of us looked smaller and further apart. There were a little over thirty-six kilometres ahead of us to finish the trek. I felt like the toughest part of the track was behind us.

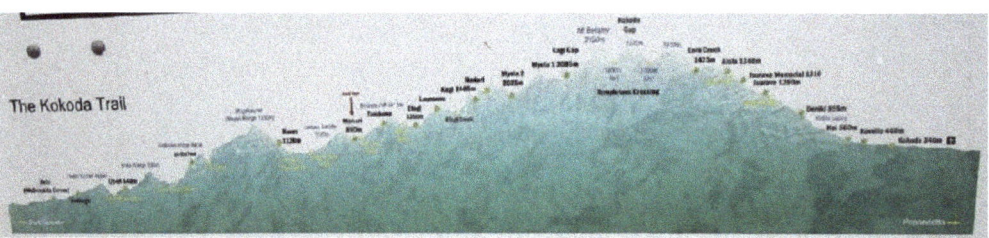

The map of the track at Menari Village.

The village ranger came over to welcome us to the village and thank us for coming to church. He hung around to chat and answer any questions we had.

"Make sure you tell everyone about the welcome you received in our village," the ranger said, echoing the words of Joel from Naduri.

On the way back to camp we found a sign and grave for Menari's last Fuzzy Wuzzy Angel[52]. He died in 2016 and was buried beside his daughter[53]. The sign said, 'The late Mr Faole Bokoi. The last Fuzzy Wuzzy Angle (sic)'.

My sandals chaffed the blisters on my little toes as I walked so I removed my shoes and walked around barefoot like the locals for the rest of the day. I actually had more grip on the muddy grass without footwear.

We located a shower with cement floor inside its own little tin shed that wasn't too far from the camp, so we were all clean by the time we ate lunch.

---

[52] We had been told Ovuru Indiki was the last Fuzzy Wuzzy, but after seeing this grave, we assumed he must have been Naduri's last.
[53] At the time of our visit, his wife still lived in the village.

The village women stopped by to braid our hair and the kids stayed to watch us. One of the girls found a clump of hair from one of us and held on to it as a souvenir. Our fine straight hair was so different from their thick, tight curls.

It started to drizzle again so we ran off to bring our clothes in from the washing line. We returned to hang out in the dining hut entertaining the kids with songs.

Matt and Rachael showed them photos on their phones. The kids showed more interest in animals and songs rather than pictures of cities. A little puppy turned up and hung around Rachael for the rest of the day.

We were running out of songs we knew the words to when Andrew suggested I do something in Japanese as I previously mentioned I knew a couple of words.

"I only know *'Mary Had a Little Lamb'* and I don't know if it's appropriate to teach them Japanese," I said.

"Yeah, Mary had a little lamb and then the Japanese killed it," Andrew said. We decided to stay away from the Japanese considering the war history of this country.

In the afternoon, the villagers carried plastic chairs from the church to our camp and set up a performance area to sing for us to raise money for the church.

After each song, the villagers all said, 'amen'. This seemed weird to us, so after a few songs we decided to clap instead. Many of the kids joined in once we started.

Our porters also sang some of their songs. During the chorus of one we'd heard several times in the last five days, the kids started giggling. This encouraged our porters to put more emphasis on those words.

"I feel like we're missing something," Andrew said.

"Yeah, I didn't realise it was a funny song," I replied.

We looked at each other trying to work out if the song was in English or Pidgin. It was a great sounding song, but we couldn't work out why it was funny.

The villagers headed off home while we ate dinner. Carla gave us the day's news explaining that working on the Sabbath would mean the person was banned from church programs such as the singing. Working three Saturdays in a row would earn a ban from the church. It surprised me that only three trekking companies stop on the Saturday so the trekking crews could attend church[54].

The map for the next day had five hours scheduled walking, but Carla predicted it would take us seven at the pace we'd been travelling, so we'd be up early to be on the track as soon as it was light enough to see.

The kids returned for more singing[55]. We got *'It's Not an Easy Road'* again, as well as a few songs with actions. There was one about a giraffe with a long neck (hold arm above head) and another about a lion with a big mane (brush hand over head) and a little waist (wiggle backside).

They sang one we all knew and could join in, although they had a couple of choruses I hadn't heard before. It started out familiar with *'if you're happy and you know it clap your hands'*. We then had *'stomp you're feet'*, *'sing a song (sha-la-la)'*, *'nod your head (ding-dong)'*, *'greet a friend'* (shake hands with people standing near you), and *'say amen (amen)'*.

It ended with *'if you're happy and you know it, do all six'*. The kids clearly had plenty of practice, but we stumbled through the last one.

"I'm getting my *'ding-dongs'* and *'amens'* mixed up," Andrew said. I nodded in agreement.

We headed off to bed by 8:30 pm. I'd done a relaxing 7,362 steps, which sounded like it was actually accurate for the first time on the trek.

---

[54] Being a personal porter to trekkers paid well and was a good way for the boys to bring money into their villages, but clearly it was at the expense of their religion if they couldn't get work with one of the three companies that respected their culture.

[55] We all pitched in a few kina to donate to their church as they were performing for us to raise money. Menari, like Naduri appeared to benefit well from trekkers. We were happy to pay them for braiding our hair and singing to us.

Day 7 – Menari to Nauro
23rd April 2017

Carla woke us at 4:30 am. Despite the early hour, we were refreshed after our rest day and all had clean clothes for the last half of the trek. The boys had made banana fritters to go with breakfast. We were packed and ready to go as the sky began to lighten.

I took back my position behind Vicko, and the puppy who hung out with us the night before trotted along beside us as we left the camp. As we headed along the track towards the church, another group approached from the left side of the track. We were more spread out than their group, so Vicko paused to let them go in front.

"Their puppy's cuter than any from our camp last night," one of them muttered.

"How many days have you been on the track?" another called out as if it was a competition to finish first.

"Every day," Matthew replied. They didn't know how to respond to that and hurried past.

We caught up to them at a log bridge not far ahead. The other team crossed first and removed their rope, before Vicko tied our rope out across the log bridge. By the time we made it to the opposite side, the other group had disappeared and we had the track to ourselves again.

The mountain ahead of us was only a 300 m ascent and on the scale of vertical to horizontal, it wasn't too bad. After close to two hours of hiking, we rested on the southern side of the peak and were rewarded with a view of Nauro Village through the clouds in the distance. It was encouraging to catch sight of our campsite so early in the morning.

Matt pulled out the map to check what lay ahead. We were excited for the two hours of level track after all the hills we had climbed only to descend again.

The next descent was called The Wall. Vicko took my camera and jogged down the slippery slope to take photos of us coming down.[56] Ben held my bag tightly as I took small careful steps.

The track began to level out and a small river lay before us. A large tree had fallen across the water with the leaves and branches at our end and the roots sticking out in all directions at the other.

The boys dropped the packs and pulled out their machetes and axes. Vicko directed them as they cut roots out of the way and felled several small trees to bridge the gap between the root system and the far bank.

While we waited on the bank, I wondered why the trekking group slightly ahead of us hadn't fixed the tree-bridge. When Vicko was satisfied with their work, the porters came back to collect the packs and help us walk across the tree trunk then along the saplings to reach the far bank.

A short distance up the track, we met the other Back Track Adventures group coming from the opposite direction. Our porters hailed theirs with shouts, shoves, and hugs.

We greeted the trekkers cheerfully as we stood aside to let their larger group pass. They didn't appear as rested as we were although they would have stopped for the Sabbath same as we did. Some were struggling, sweat dripping from foreheads as they marched wearily on, but a few returned our greeting. Several gave our freshly braided hair odd looks.

We continued on in a cheerful mood, taking it in turns to sing snippets of any songs we could recall. Unfortunately none of us were particularly good singers or great at recalling lyrics. I did manage a few verses of *'She'll be coming 'round the mountain'* though.

Occasionally, we would pass locals who stood to one side as we passed, their children swinging machetes idly as they waited. We saw children who looked as young as five years old carrying the useful jungle tool.

---

[56] None of the photos showed just how steep or muddy the terrain was in reality.

We reached the wide Brown River. Tree logs spanned from bank to bank disappearing under the water in sections, and Vicko pulled out his coil of rope once more.

We removed our boots, socks, and packs on the muddy bank, balancing on one leg to remove each sock as there was nothing clean or dry to sit on or lean against. The porters carried all our gear[57] across while we waited for our turn to cross.

The boys made a line in the river, hanging on with one hand to the log or rope to brace themselves against the fast flowing water, while leaving the other to assist us across.

I stepped out onto the log, gripping the rope with both hands while I edged along the tree trunks. The surface had notches cut into it giving my bare feet something to grip.

Halfway along, the log dipped under the water. The river tugged at me, reaching as high as my knees in places, but surprisingly it wasn't as cold as I expected. I made it to the pebbly bank on the other side and watched the rest of the group cross the river.

"How was that?" Carla asked when we were all across.

"That was fun!" we exclaimed. "From now on, we're going to call that the 'fun log'."

We took a few moments to wash the mud from our boots and gaiters, before collecting our packs and setting off in high spirits.

Ahead lay more wide, flat-ish track. In places the mud came halfway up my boots. If I stepped in a deep patch, moisture seeped through the tongue of my hiking boots, threatening to make my socks damp. The flat section was not going to be as simple as we had thought.

I had the *'It's Not an Easy Road'* song stuck in my head.

'Jesus walks beside me, and brightens the journey…'

I'm pretty sure that if he was walking beside us, he'd have lost one of his sandals in the mud.

---

[57] They took our day packs, boots and hiking poles as well as the packs they carried.

I lost my position at the front again, but I was in a better mood and found that without a pair of feet in front of me to watch, I looked up more to see where to go and noticed the scenery.

I caught up with the forward group in time to witness Rachael have what she called a 'princess moment'. We were not sure how she managed it, but her legs had been remarkably clean of mud the whole trek. Faced with a log leading into a swamp, Rachael wanted to remove her boots to keep them dry, but Vicko and the porters told her to leave them on, probably due to the fact we wouldn't be able to see what we were stepping on in the murky water.

Carla had mentioned a swamp, but on her first trek it had been almost dry. Rachael finally stepped onto the first submerged log. When it was my turn, I didn't hesitate. With my first step, water flowed over the top of my boots, soaking my socks instantly.

Ben walked in front, reaching for the upright branches that wedged the submerged logs into place to keep his balance, before turning around to hold out a hand to me.

"Step where I step," he said.

The water was muddy and I couldn't see what he stepped on, so I felt around in the swamp with my feet until I found something stable to step on.

We made it through the swamp and squelched our way along the track in soggy boots. I suddenly understood why the group we passed earlier hadn't looked as cheerful as we had.

I plodded along behind Vicko again, watching where he stepped and trying to determine if my boots in the mud made more or less noise than my wet socks in my boots. Ben fell behind and I focused on keeping my balance with each squelchy step.

To stay out of the deepest patches of mud, we walked along any tree branches laid along the track. We weaved from side to side to find the firmest path through the sludge.

Vicko stepped up onto a big fallen log and then took a large step off. I followed up onto the fallen tree. On the other side lay two smaller identical mud-covered logs. I placed my hiking poles carefully into the mud on the other side of them and stepped down.

The log gave slightly under my feet and I had a brief thought about how that must be what it feels like to step on a dead body. I almost stopped to warn Rachael behind me about the soft spot, but I'd fallen behind Vicko and I was focused on keeping my footing as I hurried after him.

"Something's not right here," Rachael called out from behind me.

She paused on the big log, poking the ground on the other side. My boot had removed some of the mud from the smaller logs revealing a pinkish colour beneath.

Matthew's porter, Pontix, leapt up out of the mud. He'd stripped down to his shorts and covered himself from head to toe in mud. He threw his arms up in the air and roared at us.

Rachael somehow managed to keep her balance on the log and the porters started laughing. Pontix raced off down the track while my brain tried to process all the thoughts going on in my mind. The main one being, so that was what stepping on a body feels like, and maybe I should have mentioned it to Rachael.

The event made me aware how easy it was for an enemy soldier to hide in this muddy jungle. I walked over Pontix's thighs and because he hadn't moved, I didn't realise he was there.

When everyone had recovered from the shock and stopped laughing, we continued on. We found Pontix at the next stream washing the mud off and getting dressed.

"Hey Rachael, you poked me in the stomach," he said. Somehow everyone seemed to forget that I'd walked over him, and Rachael copped all the teasing from the incident.

We headed uphill again until we reached the village of Nauro. They lacked the large flat plateaus of the other villages, and their huts perched on small patches of land either side of the track.

We passed the main village and stopped at a campsite set on several small terraced ledges. It would be our lunch stop as well as the evening's campsite to give us time to dry our boots.

The boys pitched the tents, several with the flap openings close to the edge of a ledge, so we'd have to be careful getting in and out of the tents in the dark.

I removed my boots and poured water out of them. The insoles I left on a bench beside my tent to dry in the sun. When I propped my boots up to dry, water pooled in the heel within moments and I had to empty them again. Eventually we placed our boots upside down on our hiking poles so the water could drain out.

We ate lunch and spent the afternoon drying clothes[58] and taking turns in the shower[59]. I pulled out a Japanese document listing various aerial bombings — the type and number of planes, the date, and whether it was reconnaissance, bombing raid, or leaflet droppings. It said, 'an enemy broadcast has stated that 80% of the troops in New Guinea are Australians'.

"There're all American planes," Matthew said as I read through the list.

After updating her trek leader paperwork, Carla stopped by the dining hut where we were gathered, to discuss the Anzac Day program. We would hold a Dawn Service at Ioribaiwa, which was the southernmost point of the track the Japanese reached in 1942, and each of us would read a section from the program she had.

Once the order was established, Carla asked if we had spare bandaids as many of the trekking crew had blisters. We dug out our spares for her to pass around.

---

[58] The blue rope came out again to act as a clothesline and we also hung our clothes over our tents to dry.

[59] The shower was a shade cloth structure, with a cement floor and a tap to turn on the cold water. It was downhill from the dining hut, so we could see the heads of the taller members of our group when they were in the shower – luckily I'm fairly short.

I had a few blisters trying to form and the tape on my feet had come loose in my wet boots. The sports tape on my knees had torn under the strain of climbing up and down the mountains.

We had another early night, going to bed by 7:45 pm. I wrote down the 18,412 steps the Garmin recorded even though I didn't believe it and fell asleep shortly afterwards.

A flat section of track. The water sat on the ground making the mud thick enough to hide in.

Part Two   Reference information
An Enemy Broadcast has stated that 80% of the troops in New Guinea are Australians, and that on the 12th April two B-17 aircraft made night time bombing raids on BUIN and the SHORTLAND ISLAND.

16th 2 aircraft Reconnaissance Raid No 33
15th 1 aircraft Reconnaissance No 36
    Salamaua, mubo area
        19th 1 B24 Bombing Raid, dropped leaflets
        18th 1 B24 Reconnaissance Raid No 31
        17th 2 B17 Reconnaissance No 32
        16th 1 B24 Bombing Raid 2 B17 Reconnaissance
        15th 1 B17 Bombing Raid, 3 P40, 2 P38 Reconnaissance

Japanese WWII document listing bombing raids carried out by American aircraft. Translations by Dugald Moyes.

Above: The muddy track winding alongside the Brown River.

Below: Entering the swamp.

Above: The 'Fun Log' crossing the Brown River.

Below: Approaching Nauro Village

Day 8 – Nauro to Ioribaiwa
24th April 2017

When I woke at 4:30 am, I had a sore throat. I added honey to both my tea and porridge. I don't normally drink much tea, but on the trek it was a good way to get some fluids in before a long day of trekking.

Day eight was another scheduled long day with two mountains to cross, so at the first hint of daylight, Danni, Nicole, and Adrian set off up the track with their porters Danny, Marcus, and Adrian.

The rest of us stood around with our packs while the last of the camp was packed up and Vicko called for us to start. We set off at 6:30 am, giving the slow group half an hour head start. My boots were still damp, but nowhere near as wet as they were the day before. With dry socks on, it wasn't too noticeable.

The morning's mountain was called Maguli Range, but after two hours of hiking up the slippery slopes with the consistency of smooth peanut butter, I re-named them the Peanut Butter Mountains.

Mud clung to our boots adding extra weight with each step. Often my foot slipped off the step above me, so I ended up back where I started. It was another slow climb placing each foot and hiking pole carefully before moving up a step. As usual, Ben was on hand to haul me up when needed.

At the top of the mountain, we encountered the rest of the group.

"We're getting cold waiting around for you," Danni joked in a repeat of several days ago when we wanted to keep moving every time they caught up to us.

The early morning sun filtered through to the mountain peak where we rested. Through a gap in the jungle, we could look out over the mountain range. Spider webs glistened with dew as they spread across the smaller plants and long grass. With Vicko in the lead, we didn't need to worry about walking into any stray webs across the track.

Nicole's phone rung, the first time there had been reception along the track[60], and then we had to wait for her to finish chatting to her partner so we could keep moving.

I fell behind the forward group after our water break and my ears became blocked. The sore throat wasn't getting any better either.

"Go slow," Ben said when I tried to increase my pace to keep up with the others. We walked alone again – too slow for the main group, but still faster than the 'slow' group. I didn't see anyone until the next rest stop.

"Are you okay? That's the longest you've taken to catch up," Andrew said.

"I'm fine," I ground out. My good mood from the day before had dissipated and I was feeling off-colour.

Descending the peanut butter mountain was just as tough as climbing it. I'd re-taped my knees and plodded along taking one step at a time. Occasionally Ben disappeared off the track and returned with flowers or brightly coloured leaves tucked into the side of his pack.

We passed a small memorial plaque on the side of the track for someone who died while trekking. Shortly afterwards, we made a small detour into the jungle where Japanese trenches[61] were still visible.

We stopped further down the track for another break. One of the porters found an unexploded mortar shell from WWII. It was so rusty after seventy-five years in the jungle it probably wouldn't explode, but one of the boys moved it away from the track anyway.

When Carla arrived, we left our packs and porters behind while one of the boys led our group off the track to Australian

---

[60] It had often been difficult to get reception with the satellite phone.

[61] The Japanese dug interconnecting trenches so they could move between them, whereas Australians dug 'fox holes' big enough for two men each. The differences made it easy to tell whose positions they were.

positions. We passed another memorial for a dead trekker. His grave stated he was only thirty-five years old when he died.

It was a harsh reminder of the difficulty of the track, seeing two memorials so close together, especially when three of our group had already been evacuated and I was unwell.

Carla pulled out her notes and gave a recap of the 1942 battle up to this point. The Japanese encountered the same supply issues the Australians had at the Kokoda end of the track. They had expected to reach Port Moresby within eleven days, but the Australians had delayed them with weeks of fierce fighting.

We listened as we stood beside holes dug by young Australian men 75 years ago. Grandad's first night spent in one of these holes was with another soldier who talked to him throughout the night to keep him calm. When the sun rose the next morning, Grandad saw that his new friend had been shot through the head. He never made friends with any of the other young men after that night.

I pulled out two translated Japanese diary entries Grandad had kept and read them to the group. They weren't appropriate to save until lunchtime when I normally shared my documents.

From the diary of Fumitoshi Yasuoka, No 1 Machine Gun Company, Tsukamoto Battalion, 18th Oct 1942, *"No provisions. Some men are said to be eating the flesh of captives. It is said to have a good flavour."*

The second one was from the diary of Lt. Sakamoto, 19th Oct 1942, *"Because of food shortage, some companies have been eating the flesh of Australian soldiers. The taste is said to be good."*

On that note, we re-joined our trekking crew on the track. To reach our lunch camp, we had a steep descent made slightly easier by rock steps placed down the side of the mountain. At the bottom was a large creek.

There was no bridge, so we removed our gaiters, boots, and socks, washed the mud off, and waded through the cold water. Ben took my boots so I had a free hand to use a hiking pole.

He held my other hand as I edged bare foot through the thigh-deep river to reach the other bank.

A few of the guys stopped for a brief swim, but the combination of the descent and the cold water made my knees ache so I didn't stay. I pulled my boots back on and climbed up the hill to the lunch hut.

I was torn between needing to sit down and having to pee. On a plateau above us was a family hut, clothesline, and toilet hut. It was a long climb up and I wondered if I could hold on.

That was when I noticed another toilet hut slightly down the hill from the dining hut. It looked easier to reach and from the location was probably the one intended for trekkers to use.

The toilet had a plastic sheet for the door and a seat, but bees swarmed around the space. I've kept bee hives in the past and I really needed to pee so I wasn't too bothered by them. When Nicole saw it, she gave it a minus-five star rating on her toilet ranking system and refused to use it.

I hiked back up to the dining hut, took off my still damp boots and socks, and lay them in the sun in the hopes they would dry properly.

By that stage, I was hot and sweating heavily. I had no appetite despite eating little for breakfast, but the boys had made a kind of spring roll with the cheese and spam. I nibbled on one and drank some Hydrolyte.

After lunch, I ended up at the back of the pack with only Ron and Carla behind me. After a short while, Danni and Nicole let Ron and me passed, but I ended up behind Adrian as we climbed the next ridge.

Despite the fact I was sick and had slowed down, Adrian still moved slower than me. I paused to let him get slightly ahead as some steps were too sloped and slippery to stop safely on.

When Adrian stopped for a breather, Ron and I moved past. I let Ron in front as he was faster, but he walked slowly so I could keep up and we chatted as we climbed. It was nice not to be automatically left behind especially when I knew he could easily catch the others with his long legs.

At one point we discovered a cluster of eucalyptus trees, the first ones we'd seen in the jungle. They made us feel like we could be back in Australia.

After another rest stop, I ended up walking with Nicole and Danni. We didn't get far when we came across one of the porters who had cut his bare foot open on a stick poking out of the mud. The guys wrapped a bandage around it so he could keep walking.

Walking with Nicole and Danni was fun. Nicole claimed her porter was a bit of a 'bad boy' as he had dreadlocks and didn't go to church on Saturday.

She had also come up with a variety of mud descriptors to add to my peanut butter mud (both smooth and crunchy varieties).

One type she called 'side mud' which made your foot slip sideways when you stepped in it. It was normally found on narrow sloped sections of track following a ridge line, so if you weren't careful you could slip off over the edge. Later we encountered one we called chocolate jaffa mud, which was like the peanut butter mud with extra chocolatey mud mixed in.

I also found out that Danny, Danni's porter, stepped on a snake earlier in the day. He was another one of the boys trekking in bare feet.

I struggled through the last two hours of hiking until we reached the village of Ioribaiwa. There were only a couple of occupied huts that we could see, but it was set on a large grassy area. The ground was reasonably dry which made a change from the previous night's cramped and muddy location.

I stopped at the tap first and removed my muddy boots and gaiters. When they were clean, I walked bare foot to where Ben had pitched my tent.

Carla set up a first aid station on the grass so she could clean and re-bandage the cut on the porter's foot and check the blisters on the other boys.

I lay down in my tent. After a while it started to drizzle, but I was too exhausted to pull down the window flap left open to air out the tent. Luckily Ron did the rounds checking the tents and closed it for me so I didn't need to move.

One of the guys called me when dinner was ready and I managed a cup of soup. Carla gave us a show and tell with some plants she collected along the track during the day. The plants included kuri grass, big leaf bamboo, and small bamboo.

Later, she pulled out a bottle of magnesium spray. She assured me would ease the pain in my knees which were beginning to swell.

I headed off to bed while the others sat around talking. I misplaced my Garmin step counter when I washed my boots at the tap so it stopped counting then. It only read 15,565 steps while Nicole's pedometer said 24,000.

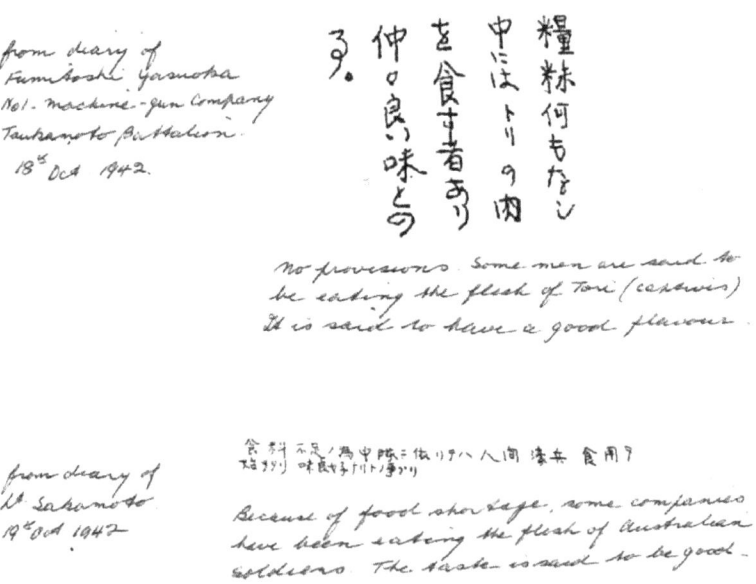

Diary entries translated by Dugald Moyes.

Above: Approaching our lunch stop. Locals had laid stones to assist with the steep descent.

Left: A blue butterfly found in several places along the track.

Above: Ioribaiwa Village – looking back up the track towards the mountain we had just climbed over.

Day 9 – Ioribaiwa to Goldie River
25th April 2017- Anzac Day

We rose at 4:30 am for the Dawn Service. I'd never done anything for Anzac Day[62] before, so it was special to be there for the 75th anniversary of the Kokoda Campaign.

My knees ached less after applying the magnesium spray the night before, but my throat was worse and I struggled to swallow. I started to sweat as soon as I crawled out of bed and began to move around, although the morning was cool.

It was still dark and the stars were out in force. I hadn't noticed many during our other nights on the track. Venus slowly rose in a bright yellow glow[63] from behind the mountain we climbed yesterday.

In the opposite direction, the mountain ridge we still had to climb was lit from behind by the bright lights of Port Moresby.

We gathered by the Ioribaiwa memorial plaque; our group to one side, the trekking crew on the other, and Carla by the memorial. Before we assembled, the boys had raised the Australian and PNG flags on their sapling poles wedged into the ground.

We took it in turns reading sections from our Dawn Service guide, recapping the battles in the area. When it was my turn, I struggled to speak around my scratchy throat, but I continued on. After my turn, Nicole read out a dedication to the Fuzzy Wuzzy Angels.

"As stretcher bearers the natives were excellent. They can get stretchers over seemingly impossible barriers and not only get them over but give the patient a comparatively comfortable ride as well. The care which

---

[62] Grandad never participated in the marches as he didn't belong to a battalion and so didn't know where to join in.
[63] It was so bright we had thought it was the moon, until Venus finally cleared the mountain peak.

they show to the patient is magnificent. Every need which they can fulfil is fulfilled. If night finds the stretcher still on the track they will find a level spot beside the track and build a shelter over the patient; they will make him as comfortable as possible, get him water and feed him if any food is available. They sleep four each side of the stretcher and if the patient moves or requires any attention during the night it is instantly given. The labour of carrying was extremely arduous but was never shirked and the natives practically never left the patient until they had brought him to his destination."[64]

In the dark, each of our porters found us, handing over a bouquet of flowers they had made from the plants they collected from the jungle the day before. They had also created a stunning wreath that Matthew laid against the battle site plaque. We stepped forward in turn to place our flowers beside it.

Ioribaiwa Ridge

Ioribaiwa Ridge, 850 metres high was the furthest southerly position reached by 5000 men of the Imperial Japanese Army in the Kokoda Campaign.

Along this East-West orientated ridge, 736 Australians withstood the advancing Japanese between the 11 and 16 September 1942. The Australian positions, some still visible as gun pits, ran from here along the ridge crest for about a kilometre in either direction and on a spur to the north. To the north-west, the ridge was little more than a razor back and hard to defend.

From 12 September the Japanese probed the more forward areas supported by mountain artillery, crossed Ofi Creek and infiltrated some Australian positions.

---

[64] Extract from the diary of Major Magarey: 2/6 Field Ambulance.

Three days later in the south-east sector the Japanese split the Australian line capturing the higher of the twin peaks.

The depleted Australian Battalions recognised this new threat. They feared a collapse and wisely withdrew on the 16 September across the featureless 6-kilometre valley on the south fully taking up new, much stronger defensive positions at Imita Ridge by 17 September.

The withdrawal, although strategically sound, was a crisis point for the Australian High Command both in Papua and Australia. There was to be no further retreat.

The Japanese were relieved to capture the ridge on the 16th but dismayed to find no Australian food supplies or materials. Japanese Headquarters, located on the southern spur of the ridge, ordered new interconnecting defence positions dug and a pause for resupply. The Japanese could see the lights of Port Moresby and 'smell victory' but no food. The Australians were now reinforced and having short supply lines harassed them repeatedly with aggressive patrols, mortars from the valley and artillery from near Owers' Corner.

Still prepared to advance, the Japanese were stunned when on the 24 September their high command ordered them to withdraw to defend the north coast. These soldiers who had fought so hard could barely believe the order but defeats on distant Guadalcanal had sealed their fate. That day the Japanese quietly withdrew, abandoning forever the dream of conquering the Owen Stanley Range.

On 28 September a carefully planned Australian advance of 2600 men entered unopposed the Japanese lines on Ioribaiwa. On the 30th Nauro was taken unopposed. The first major fight of the Australian advance was to occur twelve days later at Templeton's Crossing.

Lest We Forget

Carla played the *'Last Post'* recording that we used at Brigade Hill and then we stood in a minute silence. It was followed by the recitation of *'The Ode'* which I'd read out at Brigade Hill.

They went with songs to the battle.
They were young.
Straight of limb and true of eye,
Steady and aglow.
They were staunch to the end.
Against odds uncounted
They fell with their faces to the foe.
They shall not grow old as we that are left grow old.
Age shall not weary them, nor years condemn.
At the going down of the sun, and in the morning
We will remember them.
Lest We Forget

The porters sang several songs - one we'd heard before, but for the first time, I picked out the words:

"*Aussie, Aussie fought on this land,*
Fuzzy Wuzzy the guiding hand..."

As the sky began to lighten, we took it in turns to sing our countries' anthems, the trekking crew first and then us. We didn't stumble through it this time, having sung it days earlier for the children of Naduri.

By 6:10 am, camp was packed up and we were back on the track in the early morning light. I was not well and let the main group go ahead of me. I had no appetite, drinking only tea with honey for breakfast and nibbling on a scone with jam.

We headed downhill, but I wasn't particularly alert to my surroundings focused solely on putting one foot in front of the other as I followed Ben's heels.

At one twist in the track, I encountered 'side mud' while facing the mountain edge. For a moment I was unbalanced and unable to halt my momentum. Ben threw an arm out across my body and grabbed my arm with his other hand. I regained my balance and we continued on as though I hadn't nearly gone careening down the mountainside.

Ben made bird calls as he walked and sometimes he received a chirped reply. He stopped me at one point along the descent to point up into the towering trees, but I couldn't make out what he was trying to show me, so he kept walking. He stopped a little further ahead to point up again.

That time I caught a glimpse of the tail feathers of a Bird of Paradise. They are apparently very shy birds and not often seen. There were a couple of them in the tree tops, but it was too difficult to take a good photo through the foliage.

After some time, we stopped for a rest break and Vicko told us to swap our boots for sandals. There were nine water crossings ahead of us. From there the track wound back and forth through a series of creeks. I wasn't alert enough to count them, but there seemed to be many more than nine. We could have been crossing the same one several times.

The water was refreshing, often coming up as high as my knees, and it helped to cool me down. I stopped regularly to wash the sweat from my face.

Ben carried my boots, rinsing the mud from them in the streams. The carefully applied tape on my feet came loose and at each crossing I pocketed another piece before it washed away.

We rested for a short while in a village and I managed to eat a couple of pieces of dried fruit. Then there were a few more water crossings to wade through before we finally halted at the base of a mountain to put our boots back on.

I'd convinced myself that the last major mountain wouldn't be too bad. The village maps made it look smaller than the ones we'd conquered already, but according to our map it actually had a 600 m elevation. It rose sharply above our location by the creek.

I fell into place just ahead of the rear group and begin the slow climb up Imita Ridge. Ben slowed his pace as we quickly lost sight of the rest of the group. He stayed a couple of paces ahead, ready to give me a hand up whenever I needed it.

I started out steady, but as the mountain kept rising, I slowed to a crawl, stopping regularly to drink a few sips of water or Hydrolyte, and wipe the sweat from my face. My shirt was damp all the way through.

I slowed down until I was taking several small steps forward and coming to a stop, while Ben waited patiently for me.

Actually, that mountain didn't have a forward direction; it was just up with an occasional zigzag to the side. But I figured I must be doing alright - Ben hadn't offered to carry my bag or me yet.

I lost track of time, focused on each set of steps before I paused to catch my breath. Eventually we came out to a short flat section and Ben told me to rest. I leant against a boulder, too tired to remove my pack.

"Not far now. You can hear them up at the top," Ben said.

I looked at the track that rose sharply again, but I could made out some of the porters calling too each other ahead. I staggered to my feet and we kept walking.

The voices grew louder and I climbed up over the ridge to the cheers of the group already at the rest stop. I was severely over-heated and sweat poured off me.

The ridge was narrow, barely a few metres wide, and the ground slippery with mud. Most of the group sat on their packs to stay clean. Ben handed me a bundle of large leaves he'd pulled off nearby plants. I dropped them on the ground where I stood and collapsed on top of them.

The others congratulated me on making it to the top and asked if I was okay, but I couldn't answer them. I was close to vomiting and tears started to leak from my eyes. I poured water into the small towel from my bag and buried my head in the wet cloth.

I was still having my little meltdown, unable to stop the flow of tears, when the rear group arrived. More cheers sounded as each trekker made it over the top.

The conversation flowed around how difficult that ridge was.

"I wouldn't have made it if I hadn't asked Vicko to stop so I could eat some snacks," Rachael declared.

All I'd eaten that day were two small scones with jam, a piece of dried mango, a dried apricot, two sultanas, and two Mentos lollies. We still needed to get down off the mountain.

Several of our group wandered over to the battle site memorial plaque near where we sat. I didn't have the energy to make it over there, but I found a photo of the plaque among our group photos when we got home.

Imita Ridge

On this narrow ridge on 17 September 1942 tired Australian soldiers made their final stand to halt a relentless 8-week Japanese advance on Port Moresby. The north face of Imita is steep and Imita Gap, through which the track crosses the ridge, is approximately 850 metres above sea level.

The Australians had been strategically withdrawn from Ioribaiwa Ridge, six kilometres to the north, as Imita offered fewer places for the Japanese to manoeuvre or turn the right flank. Using only their tin helmets and bayonets, the Australians dug in and waited. Days passed. No Japanese attack came.

In those vital days, 2500 Australian reinforcements quickly reached Imita despite a gruelling five kilometre climb from the Uberi River including the 3000 wooden steps of the 'Golden Stairs'.

The Japanese by contrast were in a desperate state, behind schedule, supplies exhausted and staving. Constantly harassed by Australian patrols and mortars in the valley and artillery fire from Owers' Corner, further advance was improbable. The Japanese High Command sealed their fate on 24 September; they were ordered to withdraw silently.

On 28 September, the fresh Australian troops advanced on Imita across the valley and Ua Ule Creek to find Ioribaiwa Ridge abandoned and the Japanese in a staged retreat. The Australian counter-offensive had begun.

In this terrain supplying each army was a major problem. The Papua carriers worked for both sides but predominantly for the Australians and by October 1942, over 10000 were employed. Among the carriers were the Koiari People of this immediate area. They were also the first liberated and many emerged from hiding in the jungle to tell of their harsh treatment by the Japanese and to help the Australians.

Australian soldiers also toiled carrying a rifle with 150 rounds, two hand grenades, groundsheet, half blanket, toiletries, water bottle and food for five days. In addition to this personal 25-kilogram burden there was also the load shared with others of light mortars, machine guns and ammunition. Air-drops helped the advance but the evacuation of the wounded was a logistic nightmare.

Lest We Forget

Carla rounded the group up to go see more 'fox holes' a little way off the track. I stayed behind with Danni and Adrian who were last to reach the rest stop.

The remainder of the group hadn't been gone long when Stanley approached me.

"Are you sick?" he asked.

"Yes," I managed.

"You go with the slow group then." Stanley made the three of us get up and we made our slow descent down the other side of the ridge with our porters.

At the first stream cutting across the track, I stopped to soak my hat in the cold water and splash water on my face. I did the same thing at the next one.

I was slightly ahead of Danni and Adrian, but we were barely halfway down the ridge when Vicko overtook us with the rest of the group. They quickly disappeared out of sight.

The gradient of the ridge decreased and after what felt like hours of staggering along the track, Ben paused to point out a cleared grassy area on a nearby mountain that could be glimpsed through a break in the trees.

"That's Owers' Corner," he said.

"Yay," I said. The end was finally in sight.

"We get there tomorrow," Ben added in case I thought we had to get there that afternoon.

The plan was to camp at a site around one hour's walk from the finish line. With that new motivation, I kept plodding on.

We eventually reached a village where we stopped for lunch. I was still not hungry, so I downed more fluids and then sucked on a tube of condensed milk so I had enough energy to make it to camp.

It took about an hour to reach the Goldie River after lunch, although I couldn't tell you anything about the track in between the two locations. It was another river that required boots to be removed before wading across.

Half the group had stopped to swim before I reached the bank. Ben helped me wade through the water, before I left my gear on the bank and sat down in the river with the others. Ben hovered for a few minutes, before deciding that I wasn't moving anytime soon and he left to set up camp.

The campsite was just over the next rise, but the water was cold and helped bring my temperature down. I sat in the river until I started to get cold. I couldn't be bothered putting my boots back on, so I hiked up the rise through the mud in bare feet. I carried my boots in one hand and Matthew helped by taking my spare hiking pole. It was 3:30 pm by the time we arrived in camp. We'd been on the track for nine hours.

Ben found me and pointed me to where he'd pitched my tent. I collapsed inside, exhausted but pleased I'd made it this far on my own two legs.

Danni's porter had told her that he once had to carry his trekker all the way from Ioribaiwa to Ower's Corner, because her feet were too blistered to walk and she wanted to finish the trek rather than be evacuated.

It took a long time to find the energy to remove my wet clothes and put on clean, dry ones. It started to rain and I tucked my boots under the tent flap to keep them dry.

By the time I joined the group around the fire in the dining hut, they'd eaten all the popcorn, so I made a mug of milo and found a spot on a bench to sit. For dinner I managed a cup of beef soup and a small spoonful of fried rice.

Carla made a collection for trekking crew tips, but that involved getting money from our tents which was a muddy slope away from the dining hut. Matthew had left my spare hiking pole leaning against the hut and I offered it to Andrew so he could make it to his tent safely. He came back with mine and one of his so we could get back to our tents later.

Carla and Danni both slipped on the way to the dining hut as they weren't using poles. Somehow the porters made it over to us without the same problem when they stopped by to sing us more songs. We got *'It's Not an Easy Road'* again and my new favourite, *'Aussie Aussie'*.

I made it to bed by 8:30 pm. Garmin said I'd only done 15,893 step although it felt like at least double that just to make it up Imita Ridge. It would be going into the back of a drawer as soon as I got home.

Left: Anzac Day wreath and bouquets made for us by the PNG boys.

Above: The track winding along the left side of one of the many water crossings.

Below: A brief flat section – peering back down Imita Ridge.

Day 10 – Goldie River to Ower's Corner
26th April 2017

I woke briefly at 4:20 am struggling to swallow around my sore throat. I drifted back to sleep before waking again as the sky began to lighten.

We'd run out of tea bags, so I scraped the last half a teaspoon of milo into a mug and added honey and condensed milk. The concoction was sweet enough to give a person diabetes, but I drank it down to give me the energy to walk the last hour of the track.

Vicko did his last *'Rock and Roll'* call and we set off at 7:10 am. We climbed another hill, but it wasn't ridiculously steep. I lost everyone again, except Ben, as I stumbled up the track.

As much as I had enjoyed the experience of hiking across the mountain range where Grandad had spent time during WWII, I was relieved it was almost over. I wanted to lie down and take something soothing for my throat. My ears unblocking would have been nice as well. I spared a thought for all the soldiers who had walked the track while sick or wounded during the war. Grandad had contracted malaria at one point. We all took tablets to prevent the same happening to us.

After about an hour I caught up to where Vicko, Matt, Rachael, and Andrew waited. Ben disappeared up the track with the other porters. We waited as everyone joined us and the trekking crew headed off.

Matt and Rachael squabbled good-naturedly about who would get to be in front for the final leg of the trek, but in the end Vicko said slow people first. I fell in behind Danni and Adrian.

"Are you part of the slow group now?" Rachael asked.

"I have been for the last two days," I replied.

"How much longer?" someone asked.

"Fifteen more minutes," Vicko said.

"So forty-five minutes for me," Danni joked. Her porter, Danny had been telling her much longer time frames than everyone else for days.

We started walking, but Vicko stopped us for a water break barely five minutes later. We suspected it was to give the trekking crew time to get in place to welcome us across the finish line.

We paused again before we reached the top. The top of a tall tree at the finish line could be seen above the rise. Behind us lay a spectacular view of the mountain range we had spent the last nine days crossing.

Finally, Vicko led us over the rise. The trekking crew made a guard of honour on either side of the Kokoda Track[65] arch. We walked through the PNG and Australian flags as we crossed the finish to the sound of the boys singing.

Ten of our original group of thirteen (not including the twenty PNG boys) completed the trek. We congratulated Carla on her skills as Trek Leader and jokingly pointed out that she hadn't lost any of us after she took over from Martin.

"There were some easy days and some hard days," Nicole said.

"Was the easy day the Sabbath?" I asked.

She laughed and nodded her head. "Yes."

Kokoda Trail
Papua New Guinea

The Japanese attack on Port Moresby in May 1942 was repulsed at the Battle of the Coral Sea, a month later the navy was severely damaged at the Battle of Midway. These events prompted another approach to Port Moresby and on 22 July, 2,000 Japanese were landed near Gona with the aim of crossing the Owen Stanley Range via the tortuous Kokoda Trail (Track).

---

[65] It read 'Kokoda Track' on one side and 'Kokoda Trail' on the other as no one seemed to agree on which one it should be called.

During the next week 80 Australians and Papuans fought delaying actions, culminating in a battle at Kokoda Village. The Japanese force rose to 10,000 whilst advancing along the Kokoda Trail. They were constantly delayed by defensive action particularly at Isurava and Brigade Hill. However, by mid September the Australians (reduced from 3,000 to 300 men) were forced back to Imita Ridge, 42 km from Moresby.

The Japanese were then ordered to withdraw as their 5,000 remaining men and supplies were totally exhausted, and their army at Guadalcanal (Solomon Islands) was on the defensive against the Americans.

On 23 September the Australians, now 2,600 strong, moved northwards to recover the trail. Encountering major opposition only at Templeton's and Eora Creek, Kokoda was entered unopposed on 2 November. The Japanese rearguard was destroyed near Gorari. 5,000 Japanese survived and joined 4,000 fresh troops around Gona and Buna. Australian and American forces captured these strongholds by January 1943, incurring heavy casualties on both sides.

The Papuan carriers played an important role in the defence of the Kokoda Trail. They transported Australian casualties and supplies. Their loyalty will be remembered forever.

Owers' Corner

The Kokoda Trail begins in the foothills of the Owen Stanley Mountain Range at Owers' Corner. Here the mountain range looms over the rough jungle road from Sogeri as it gave way to a narrow rapidly descending footpath. Captain Noel Owers of the New Guinea Volunteer Rifles mapped parts of the track just before the Japanese invasion and hence its name.

Kokoda Village is at the end of the track. It is 96 kilometres away but with over 5,500 metres of climbing it takes 10 days by foot.

In 1942 ammunition and supplies were trucked 45 kilometres from Port Moresby to Owers' where they were repacked in 70 kg loads. These were transported by horse or mule to Uberi, a major supply base just beyond the Goldie River. From Uberi only sure-footed native carriers were able to traverse the tortuous track ahead.

Two artillery pieces were dragged to Owers' to give support to the Australians fighting the Japanese on Ioribaiwa Ridge.

Owers' Corner can be the beginning, today, of a great adventure or the goal of a weary hiker. However for many brave men this was their last contact with civilisation. As you pass, please remember them.

Lest We Forget

Ower's Corner looking back over the mountains we crossed.

All amounts are estimates only	Total	Killed	Wounded
Australians Kokoda Trail Buna-Gona	7,500 12,000	625 1,540	1,055 2,478
Papuans Kokoda & Buna-Gona	10,000	Unknown	
United States of America Kokoda Trail Buna-Gona	Nil 15,000	Nil 930	Nil 1918
Japanese Kokoda Trail Gona-Buna	13,500 9,000	12,000 (combined)	2,000 evacuated by sea 3,400 escaped
Incidence of sickness 3 times that of battle casualties			

    The Kokoda Track arch displayed plaques dedicated to the six[66] Australian states, listing which battalions came from that location. Another was dedicated to the PNG units.

    We said goodbye to our trekking crew. Some would walk home from here, others had business in Port Moresby. Pontix, Matthew's porter was 25 years old and about to start his final year of high school. We took it for granted that we could easily reach a school, but it wasn't so easy for those who live in third world countries.

    Trekking provided the villagers with work and an opportunity to go to school. It would also give Pontix's cut foot time to heal before he made the trek again. We did discover though, that these boys could complete the track in two days if not laden down with a pack and a slow Australian.

---

[66] Northern Territory was not included.

We piled onto a bus and drove down the road until we reached the McDonald's Corner memorial. A white-painted, wire statue of a soldier, in a helmet and holding a bayonet, stood in a small clearing beside a rubber plantation. A plaque sat at its base:

> This monument commemorates the exploits of the 39th Infantry Battalion who were first to engage the Japanese along the Kokoda Trail in 1942. To honour the 138 members who gave their lives in New Guinea and in remembrance of P.J.McDonald their true and loyal friend.

We got back on the bus for the trip to Port Moresby. On the way, we stopped at the Bomana War Cemetery, the largest in the Pacific area.

Row after row of white headstones lined the lawn. Some had the soldier's name and unit listed, others stated *'an Australian soldier of the 1939-1945 war † known to God'*. Some merely stated, *'a soldier of the 1939-1945 war † known to God'*, if it was likely they weren't Australian.

Above us sat a circular pavilion with plaques listing the names of those whose bodies hadn't been recovered. The names were listed by their unit.

We finished our Kokoda experience with another service on the lawns of the cemetery to remember all those who fought for our freedom during WWII.

Bomana War Cemetery, Port Moresby

About the Trek

I was in Port Moresby, Papua New Guinea for work in December 2016, and it made me curious about Grandad's war service. All I knew was he'd been in Port Moresby at one point, was a translator, and learned to speak Japanese from a POW.

When I got back to Australia, I called my siblings. I discovered Grandad had been on the Kokoda Track (also known as the Kokoda Trail) in 1942 and my brother had documents from Grandad's time during the war, including several that looked like they were from the War Trials.

It was difficult to work out exactly where Grandad had been as he didn't belong to a battalion. The Allied Translator and Interpreter Service was formed in August 1942 and initially consisted of only twenty-five people. From what I could tell, Dugald Moyes joined the Kokoda Campaign with the fresh Australian troops as they made their advance up back up the track to re-capture Kokoda.

Grandad would later translate for the Americans, go to the Philippines, and then to the War Trials held in Rabaul at the conclusion of WWII. He was finally released from service in 1946 when he received news of his father's death back in Australia.

One of his frustrations during the war was that he translated many useful documents, much coming from the diaries of the Japanese, which was ignored by his superiors. The commanders believed the information to be fake, as it was too easy to find. It was later discovered that the Japanese didn't believe anyone could read their language and the information was real.

This lead to a lifetime dislike of bureaucrats. And Americans. Our allies didn't make a favourable impression on the Australians soldiers.

Many Australians were resentful of the delay with the Americans joining the campaign. The vastly outnumbered

Australians battled the superior Japanese force on their own and according to Grandad, it became a joke among the men that the Americans were 'waiting for their icecream' before joining the fight.

Surprisingly, despite not having any time for Americans, I only ever heard Grandad say one thing against the Japanese in my whole life. He always enjoyed testing his language skills when meeting a Japanese tourist or language teacher in Australia.

I learned a lot of Australian war history while preparing for and trekking the Kokoda Track, but the area was so much more than its past. I've mentioned a fair amount of history surrounding the track due to Grandad's connection to the place, but even without that, the track would have been an incredible place to hike.

The track was a challenge, a test of fitness. Six people have died on the track since 2001[67] and around fifty people are evacuated by the *'Hunger Games'* helicopter every trekking season. We heard the helicopter several times every day we were on the track.

Besides that, the scenery was incredible. The jungle was dense, but when you came out to a clearing, you were rewarded with amazing mountain views. It was truly a beautiful place.

For those who love botany, the jungle was sprinkled with incredible flowers and plant life, evident in the wreath and flower bouquets we received throughout the trek.

You definitely need to be fit for this trek, but if you've ever thought about walking the Kokoda Track or just love challenging treks through beautiful scenery, give it a go.

I'd like to thank Back Track Adventures for an incredible experience. I would definitely recommend them to anyone considering the trek. They are one of only three companies that currently stop trekking on the Sabbath and although I'm

---

[67] A further nine died in a plane crash on the way to Kokoda.

not religious, it was a great experience to spend a whole day with the villagers and we were well rested for the second half of the trek. They also took care of all the extra site fees along the track so we didn't need to worry about having additional money for those times.

Another thank you to the PNG trekking crew and in particular my porter Ben who kept me on my feet the whole trek. I only landed on my bum once. The boys demonstrated the dedication and loyalty of their Fuzzy Wuzzy Angel ancestors.

Finally to my trekking group who made the trip extra special. We were there to raise money for Lifeline and Beyondblue charities, which was really successful. They were a fun and supportive group to take on this challenge with. Our trainee trek leader also did an amazing job, after our leader was evacuated.

Now every Anzac Day, I can look back and remember walking this track on the 75th anniversary of the WWII Kokoda Campaign.

About the Author

Nikki Moyes was born in Victoria and has moved around Australia amassing an eclectic range of occupations including tall-ship watch leader, apiarist, rose farm hand, and sandwich artist. In her spare time she learns tissu, static trapeze, and aerial hoop (she couldn't decide on one) in case she needs to run off and join the circus.

You can find her here:
www.facebook.com/moyes.nikki/
twitter: @NikkiNovelist
www.goodreads.com/author/show/15606198.Nikki_Moyes

Other books by Nikki Moyes

Young Adult Fiction:

If I Wake

Will is sixteen year old Lucy's best friend. Their lives intersect in dreams, where destiny pulls them together through different times in history. Even though their meetings are more real to Lucy than the present, Lucy is uncertain if Will exists outside her mind. Lucy's mum thinks there is something wrong when Lucy sleeps for days at a time. She is so caught up with finding a cure she doesn't see the real problem. Lucy is bullied at school and is thinking of ending her life. When the bullying goes too far and Lucy ends up in a coma, only Will can reach her. But how do you live when the only person who can save you doesn't exist?

www.ingramcontent.com/pod-product-compliance
Lightning Source LLC
Chambersburg PA
CBHW062111290426
44110CB00023B/2779